Calabash chicken shaddock salad

MARY SLATER

CARIBBEAN COOKING

HAMLYN

Illustrated by Gay John Galsworthy

First published in 1970 as *Caribbean Cooking for Pleasure*

This edition published in 1984 by Hamlyn
an imprint of Reed Consumer Books Limited
Michelin House, 81 Fulham Road, London SW3 6RB
and Auckland, Melbourne, Singapore and Toronto

Reprinted 1985, 1988, 1994

ISBN 0 600 34731 1

A CIP catalogue record for this book is available from
the British Library

Printed in Hong Kong

CONTENTS

INTRODUCTION

West Indian legend has it that as earliest man wandered starving through the steaming savannah, the Carib god, Kabo Tano, took pity on him and created a great tree, a tree hung with all the fruits and foods he would need; sapodillas, mangoes, coconuts, pawpaw and cassava. Every man cut himself a branch and so it is that, today, food grows near almost every Caribbean home.

In my island garden, guavas, golden apples, pomegranates, limes and breadfruit fall amid a tangle of flowers. One cannot say when they will be in season; in perpetual summer, ripening depends largely on rainfall. Sometimes fruits, appear after eight months, sometimes a tree takes a full year to bear again; once 'sweet' as the expression is, down come the birds and monkeys, not to mention local children, stripping the fruit almost before it can be gathered for jam and preserves. As the sun shines all the year round, islands of plenty (those with mountains and rain forests) produce all the time, flat coral islands, atolls with thin top soil, rarely have abundance but import from their neighbours.

In the great arc of islands stretching from Florida in the North, down through the Bahamas in the Atlantic to the South American mainland, every one is utterly different, some thick with flowers and trees, others volcanic, barren and craggy. To say one knows the West Indies one must know almost every island. Each derives characteristics from the historical past with its conquest and colonisation. In some cases, the islands have changed hands between nations, not once, but several times. Some have French, Dutch, Spanish, American or British customs and Danes, Portuguese, Indians, Lebanese and Chinese, all mix and mingle with the Africans who form the bulk of the West Indian population. There is no distinct trend in Caribbean cooking, many nations brought and left their customs, habits and ceremonies just as they left their regional dishes.

Some traditional cooking is, frankly, heavy and unattractive to cosmopolitan palates, other dishes are delicious and should be tried by visitors. In this book, I do not set out to list the regional recipes but to choose those with the widest appeal, and I have endeavoured to suggest some new ways, possibly my ways, of using Caribbean produce rather than adding yet another title to the books of traditional recipes which already exist.

I urge all visitors to the Caribbean to sample the unfamiliar while enjoying the familiar food offered in most hotels. The day I wrote this page, a small boy, holidaying in the islands for the fourth time with his parents, came into my kitchen and saw a pawpaw, one of the most abundant of tropical fruits, ripening on a shelf. "What's that?", he enquired, never having been given a taste, never having gone beyond hotel grounds and beach into the colourful, noisy markets or into the country where such fruits grow everywhere.

Many hotels offer 'efficiency' apartments, suites or cottages with kitchens where visitors can, if they wish, prepare some of their own food. This arrangement offers delightful freedom from mealtime routine as well as the opportunity of trying local produce. It is rewarding to cook the fish which lashed on the line a short half hour before; but marketing can be confusing, as fruit and vegetables are not only unfamiliar but their names vary from island to island.

Islanders know exactly how fish should be prepared – fresh from the sea with a good squeeze of lime. Père Labat, in his famous travelogue written in 1724, devotes almost a chapter to titiri, tiny fish smaller than whitebait. Banana dishes are endless, aflame in rum or as banana bread, a tea time change which can be made by housewives almost anywhere in the world. Coconuts make candy, cream or the basis of many drinks. Last time I was in St. Lucia I noticed a factory producing coconut crisps, grilled and packed like potato crisps. Breadfruit is just what

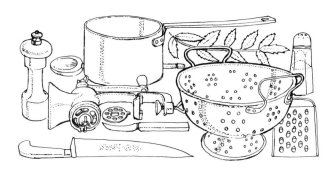

it sounds like, a staple food, toasted and buttered or boiled, mashed or sliced. One of the chief reasons for the mutiny on the *Bounty* was because Captain 'Breadfruit' Bligh lavished more care on his sapling trees than on his crew, but islanders have since had cause to be thankful for his precious cargo from which an important item of their diet sprang. The original tree, planted by Captain Bligh, can be seen in Kingstown Botanic Garden, St. Vincent. Shiny green breadfruit leaves are so decorative they are sometimes used as table mats and the huge fruit, weighing as much as four pounds, is seen in every market.

The plantocracy, as old time wealthy planters were called, were by no means tyrants. Anxious to keep their essential labour force contented and healthy, they imported foods from Africa, Spain and North America. In the very early days, soon after discovery by Columbus, European settlers brought crops from the Old World and although some failed, fruit immediately flourished. Figs, oranges and lemons came from Spain, bananas and pineapples came from the Canaries with Canary Islanders to instruct in their cultivation. Later, the fabulous wealth of the planters derived from sugar; from sugar came rum, 'Kill-devil', the spirit of cane, which remains the drink of the Caribbean islands to this day.

Most books on the Caribbean begin with quotations from the letters written by Columbus to his king, Ferdinand of Spain, full of vivid descriptions of the lands and peoples he discovered. 'Darkly green . . . the fairest island that eyes have beheld', he wrote of Jamaica in 1494 and, if the absence of hoped-for gold and his later shipwreck and misadventures were to leave him with few happy memories, Caribbean beauty was never disputed. Among widely read accounts of those early days of conquest and settlement are Oviedo's 'General History of the Indies' (1539) Las Casas in his 'Short Account of the Destruction of the Indies' (1552), a passionate denunciation of the cruelty of the Spanish *conquistadors*. Père Labat, writing later, gives picturesque and humorous details of life in the French West Indies with many a gastronomic note: the good priest relished his food!

Of the British islands, much is learned from Maria Nugent, a Governor's wife (1801) who kept a detailed journal of her time in Jamaica, and Mathew 'Monk' Lewis (1805-1817) in his 'Journal of a West Indian Proprietor', Anthony Trollope follows with 'The West Indies and Spanish Main' (1859). All refer to the foods they ate, the mounds of colour spilling from the vendors' baskets, to turtle, crayfish, tree oysters and to conch "They put a little fire to the shell and it instantly left its dwelling, poor little fish", wrote Lady Nugent, and I find that putting it on ice does exactly the same thing. Except for the festal sucking pig, the meat of the islands is unremarkable but in the cooking it often becomes spicy, fiery and exciting.

To housekeep in the Caribbean, for longer or shorter periods, is to exercise infinite patience, to forget time and enjoy the beauty and colour that lies all around, to learn to appreciate the smiling people, to know something of their origin and traditions. Each time I go back to the islands I think of a saying I once heard, "When God made the earth he kept this bit for himself".

Mary Slater, St. Peter, Barbados

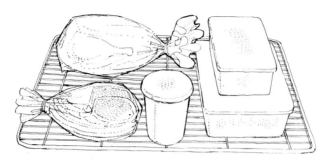

WEIGHTS AND MEASURES

Weights throughout the book are given in lb. and oz. Liquid measure is in Imperial pints and fractions thereof, with small amounts in spoon measures. For the benefit of American readers liquid ingredients have been given to the nearest U.S. standard cup measure. These follow the English measure, i.e. 1 pint (U.S. $2\frac{1}{2}$ cups).

All spoon measures refer to the British Standards Institution specification. All measures are levelled off to the rim of the spoon. To measure fractions of spoons use the small measures provided in measuring sets or divide the level spoon. The

American standard measuring spoons are slightly smaller in capacity than the British standard measuring spoons. The proportion however is similar in that 3 American standard teaspoons equal 1 tablespoon.

BRITISH	AMERICAN
1 teaspoon	1 teaspoon
1 tablespoon	1 tablespoon
2 tablespoons	3 tablespoons
$3\frac{1}{2}$ tablespoons	4 tablespoons
4 tablespoons	5 tablespoons

HANDY CONVERSION TABLE

ENGLISH MEASURE	(Approximate conversion table)	AMERICAN CUPS
1 lb.	Butter or other fat	2 cups
1 lb.	Flour (sifted)	4 cups
1 lb.	Granulated or Castor Sugar	$2\frac{1}{4}$ cups
1 lb.	Confectioners' or Icing Sugar	$3\frac{1}{2}$ cups
1 lb.	Brown Sugar (moist)	$2\frac{1}{4}$ cups
1 lb.	Golden Syrup or Treacle	$1\frac{1}{3}$ cups
1 lb.	Rice	$2\frac{1}{4} - 2\frac{1}{2}$ cups
1 lb.	Dried Fruit (chopped)	3 cups
1 lb.	Raw Chopped Meat (finely packed)	2 cups
1 lb.	Lentils or Split Peas	2 cups

1 lb.	Coffee (unground)	$2\frac{1}{2}$ cups
1 lb.	Dry Breadcrumbs	4 cups
8 oz.	Butter or other fat	1 cup
8 oz.	Lard	1 cup
7 oz.	Castor Sugar	1 cup
7 oz.	Soft Brown Sugar	1 cup (packed)
6 oz.	Candied Fruit	1 cup
$6\frac{1}{3}$ oz.	Chopped Dates	1 cup
6 oz.	Chocolate Pieces	1 cup
6 oz.	Currants	1 cup
$5\frac{1}{2}$ oz.	Cooked Rice	1 cup
$5\frac{3}{4}$ oz.	Seedless Raisins	1 cup
5 oz.	Candied Peel	1 cup
4 oz.	Chopped Mixed Nuts	1 cup
5 oz.	Sliced Apple	1 cup
$4\frac{1}{2}$ oz.	Icing Sugar	1 cup (sifted)
4 oz.	Cheddar Cheese	1 cup (grated)
$3\frac{1}{2}$ oz.	Cocoa	1 cup
3 oz.	Desiccated Coconut	1 cup

2 oz.	Fresh Breadcrumbs	1 cup		$\frac{1}{2}$ oz.	Flour	2 tablespoons*
				1 oz.	Flour	$\frac{1}{4}$ cup
1 oz.	Plain Dessert Chocolate	1 square		1 oz.	Sugar	2 tablespoons
$\frac{1}{4}$ oz.	Dried Yeast	1 packet		$\frac{1}{2}$ oz.	Butter	1 tablespoon smoothed off
$\frac{1}{4}$ oz.	Gelatine	1 tablespoon				
$\frac{3}{4}$ tablespoon	Gelatine	1 envelope		1 oz.	Golden Syrup or Treacle	1 tablespoon
				1 oz.	Jam or Jelly	1 tablespoon

* must be standard U.S. measuring tablespoon

NOTES ON METRICATION

Exact conversion from Imperial to metric measures does not usually give very convenient working quantities and so the metric measures have been rounded off. The tables below show the recommended equivalents.

Solid measures

Ounces	Recommended gram conversion to nearest unit of 25
1	25
2	50
3	75
4	100
5	150
6	175
7	200
8	225
9	250
10	275
11	300
12	350
13	375
14	400
15	425
16 (1 lb.)	450

Liquid measures

Imperial	Recommended ml.
$\frac{1}{4}$ pint	150 ml.
$\frac{1}{2}$ pint	300 ml.
$\frac{3}{4}$ pint	450 ml.
1 pint	600 ml.
$1\frac{1}{2}$ pints	900 ml.
$1\frac{3}{4}$ pints	1000 ml. (1 litre)
$2\frac{3}{4}$ pints	1·5 litres
$3\frac{1}{2}$ pints	2 litres

Oven temperatures

The table below gives recommended equivalents.

	°F	°C	GAS MARK
Very cool or very slow	225	110	$\frac{1}{4}$
	250	120	$\frac{1}{2}$
Cool or slow	275	140	1
	300	150	2
Moderate	325	160	3
	350	180	4
Moderately hot	375	190	5
	400	200	6
Hot	425	220	7
	450	230	8
Very hot	475	240	9

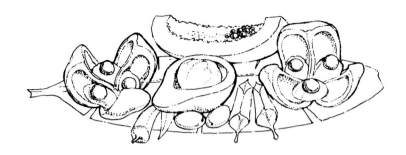

GLOSSARY

In the tropics, perishable foods, meat, fish, cheese, eggs, milk and so on, should be stored in a refrigerator; bread keeps fresh for days, if tightly tied in a plastic bag and kept in the 'fridge' Vegetables should be stored in the 'fridge' or on a tiered metal rack; fruit should be allowed to ripen before refrigeration, and should not be allowed to freeze or the flavour is lost; remove some time before serving. Most tropical fruits taste best when warmed by the sun, the way they were intended to be eaten.

Some of the best furniture is the kind which stands on legs; this may appear old fashioned, but the legs can be placed in jars full of water which prevents the onset of ants. The water should be topped up from time to time. Newcomers to the tropics should remember that food cannot be left exposed, no matter how small the amount, or there will be a line of ants marching in that direction within minutes.

A useful aid to tropical shopping is an insulated bag with several packs of dry ice. The packs should be frozen in the refrigerator and will keep frozen for several hours if wrapped in a plastic bag.

LOCAL COOKING UTENSILS

Canarees, earthenware pie dishes and casseroles.
Coalpots, of iron or clay, used in the country, and for traditional stews and pepperpots requiring prolonged cooking.
Pestles and mortars; very large ones are found in stores and homes; these are used for pounding foods.
Water coolers, made of glazed earthenware, are useful in kitchens and workrooms.
Yabbas, glazed clay pots used in the country for cooking, mixing and storage.

FISH AND SHELLFISH

BONITO, a game fish which weighs up to 12 lb.

BUTTER FISH, an inshore fish, netted in schools which weighs about 8 oz.

CALEPEAVE, a river fish, not unlike salmon.

CRAYFISH, a crustacean, with no claws, small and more colourful than a lobster with a very delicious flesh.

CONCH, a mollusc which varies in size up to a foot long; some are deep magenta, others a delicate pink and a few contain a lustreless pink pearl.

CUTLASS, a ribbon-like fish whose small bones must be filleted with care.

DOLPHIN, a game fish which swims near the surface; an excellent culinary fish which can weigh up to 30 lb.

FLYING FISH, taxi on the surface when escaping large fish; they have wing-like fins and weigh about 8 oz.

GROUPER, a game fish feeding offshore which weighs about 8 lb.; the flavour is similar to bass.

JACK, several fish go by this name, varying in size from 8 oz. to 3 lb.; there is the 'goggle-eye' and the 'horse-eye' and some are known as 'married women'.

JONGA, a river fish.

KINGFISH, a game fish, sometimes called King Mackerel which can weigh up to 100 lb.; rather tasteless unless well prepared.

MACKEREL, sometimes called kingfish, but much smaller than the true kingfish only about 1-3 lb.

MARLIN, one of the most sought-after game fish, found in rocks and reefs, sometimes called the 'white fox' or 'big daddy'.

MULLETT, found offshore, feeds on marine plants and weighs about 1½-3 lb.

OYSTER, the tree variety are found in mangrove swamps; the shell has spines which cling to the trees.

SAILFISH, a game fish, found in schools; the high dorsal fin has the appearance of a sail.

SHARK, a game fish which varies in size; the edible parts are very tasty.

SNAPPER OR REDFISH, usually caught offshore, feeds on crabs and small fish; an excellent culinary fish which weighs about 6-8 lb.

TARPON, a game fish with a sail-like fin and short, sharp teeth; can weigh up to 60 lb.

TITIRI, tiny fish, smaller than whitebait netted in the Eastern Caribbean.

TUNA, a game fish, sometimes weighing as much as 120 lb.; an excellent culinary fish.

TURTLE, the green variety is most often eaten, but is dying out. Some islands, such as Grand Cayman, are experimenting with breeding in captivity.

WHELK, an edible scavenger; the shell measures 1 – 5 inches.

Note
Crabs, lobsters, shrimps and prawns are found on many beaches.

VEGETABLES

ACKEE, grows on trees and is so plentiful in Jamaica it is called 'free food'. Very poisonous when unripe, when ripe, the fruit splits to show three large black seeds; the yellowish flesh, when cooked, looks something like scrambled eggs.

ARTICHOKE, both globe and Jerusalem are found.

AUBERGINE, usually known as egg plant, garden egg or melongene.

BHAGI, a weed, not unlike spinach, used in Indian dishes.

BREADFRUIT, a large rough skinned vegetable, which grows on trees and can weigh up to 4 lb.; it is one of the staple foods of the islands.

CABBAGE, the same as the European and American kinds.

CALLALOO OR CALALU the leaves of the eddo, a green vegetable not unlike spinach.

CARROT, the same as the European and American kinds.

CASSAVA, a thin root containing prussic acid which must be grated, boiled or roasted to extract the poison. It then becomes a flour when ground and makes 'bammies', 'cassava bread) and various other other farinaceous dishes.

CHOCHO, see cristophene.

COCO, see eddo.

CRISTOPHENE, sometimes spelt christophine, a pear-shaped member of the melon family with pale green skin and flesh which tastes something like marrow.

CUSH CUSH, one of the best varieties of yam.

DASHEEN, see eddo.

EDDO, a hairy root about the size of a large potato and not unlike in taste.

ESCHALOT OR ESCALLION, very small spring onions or chives.

LETTUCE, island grown, tend to be thin with serrated brown-edged leaves.

MUSHROOMS, found on some islands.

OKRA OR OCHRA, a spear shaped green pod filled with glutinous seeds; when large it is too fibrous to eat. The basis of 'gumbo' dishes and eaten with rice by the islanders.

PEA, various types, black-eye, chick and 'gunga' (congo). What is called 'pea' in Jamaica is a red or kidney bean.

PLANTAIN, like a large banana, but must be cooked.

PUMPKIN, often called by the American name, squash.

POTATO, means SWEET POTATO; there are various kinds, some brown and some red skinned. Unsweet potatoes are called ENGLISH or IRISH POTATOES.

SORREL, like a sour version of spinach. The green leaves can be chopped and used as flavouring, in salads or for soup. The fruit sepals, left after the flower petals drop, are red.

TANNIA, similar to an eddoe.

TOMATO, the same as European and American varieties, but often yellow when ripe.

TOPI TAMBO, looks like a small potato but tastes like a Jerusalem artichoke.

WATERCRESS, found on a few islands.

YAM, a brown hairy root like a potato.

FRUITS AND NUTS

AVOCADO, green or purple skinned, usually simply called 'pear'.

BANANA, often called 'fig', especially the small variety. Fig bluggoes, rust skinned, are for cooking.

BARBADOS CHERRY, not unlike the European white cherry in appearance but too sharp to eat raw; used for jam.

CASHEW, kidney-shaped fruit, yellow or red when ripe; the juice is used for jelly or soft drinks and the kernel yields cashew nuts.

COCONUT, used unripe (green) and ripe (brown). The white meat of the ripe coconut is used grated, toasted or flaked and the milk made into cream. Green coconuts contain jelly and water.

CUSTARD APPLE, a brown fruit with sweet, moist pulp, cream coloured like custard.

GRAPEFRUIT, the same as the European citrus.

GRENADILLA, fruit about the size of a small melon, which grows on a vine; used as flavouring for soft drinks and desserts.

GINEP, small green fruit with apricot-coloured flesh and one large stone.

GUAVA, small yellow-skinned fruit with pink or yellow flesh and many seeds, Can be eaten raw, stewed or made into jelly or 'cheese', a paste, usually cut into squares.

HOG PLUM, about the size of a European plum, pleasantly flavoured can be eaten raw or made into jam.

LEMON, very similar to European citrus, but often rough skinned.

LIME, smooth-skinned citrus, smaller than a lemon.

MAMMEE APPLE, an oval fruit with rough brown skin and apricot-coloured flesh tasting something like apricot, with several large seeds. Can be eaten raw or stewed.

MANGO, grows on large trees, a fruit with greenish-yellow skin, very sweet tasting apricot-coloured pulp, and a large stone. Smaller types are stringy but larger varieties, Julies and Bombays are smooth and delicate. Unripe, they can be used for chutney.

MELON, both cantaloup and pink-fleshed water melons.

OTAHEITE APPLE, a pear-shaped fruit with polished bright red skin, pretty but rather tasteless. The white flesh is used mainly for cooking and jam.

ORTANIQUE, tangerine crossed with orange which originated in Jamaica.

PAWPAW, OR PAPAYA, varies in size and flavour. Skin is greenish or yellow when very ripe, flesh apricot coloured and delicate; centre filled with peppery black seeds. The pulp contains pepsin and the skin and seeds are useful as meat tenderisers; when unripe, it can be used as a vegetable.

PINEAPPLE, various sizes, plentiful on some islands.

SAPODILLA OR NASEBERRY, fruit about the size of a large plum, brown skinned with sweet, yellowish flesh and several large flat black seeds.

SEA OR BAY GRAPE, grows in clusters like the European grape, but is acid and suitable only for jam or jelly.

SHADDOCK, pink-fleshed grapefruit.

SORREL, a plant whose sepals, left when the flower petals drop, are red and fleshy; used as a drink, or for jelly and jam.

SOURSOP, a large, green-skinned fruit covered in soft spines. The rather acid white flesh has many black, shiny seeds in the centre; sieved, it makes a creamy drink or ice cream.

STAR APPLE, a purple-skinned fruit which must be picked and ripened off the tree. The white flesh is rather tasteless and the pips are arranged in star formation; mixed with orange it makes a pleasant dessert.

SUGAR APPLE OR SWEETSOP, has a skin covered with rubbery scales, often with a bloom on them. The flesh is creamy, sweet and pleasant.

TAMARIND, a long brown pod which becomes sweet and brittle when ripe, cracking to expose black seeds.

TANGERINE, large and sweet on some islands. In Jamaica, where they are plentiful, boys tie them to sticks and sell them by the mountain roadside.

UGLI FRUIT, a large citrus, uneven and thick skinned, not unlike a grapefruit when peeled.

Note
In the Caribbean islands, one always speaks of FRUITS (plural) never FRUIT. If any is picked or bought unripe, it is sweeter and ripens more quickly if wrapped in a paper bag rather than leaving it in a sunny place. In any recipe lemon juice can be used in place of lime.

HERBS, SPICES AND SEASONINGS

ALLSPICE, so called because it smells slightly of nutmeg, cinnamon and cloves. The berry, the size of a pea, is glossy black when ripe; used in sweet chutneys, curries and marinades.

BAY, an evergreen with dark green leaves; used in soups, stews and for *bouquet garni*.

CASSAREEP, made from cassava juice; used for traditional stews and pepperpots.

CHIVE, similar to spring onion, but the flavour is more delicate; used chopped, in salads, fish, omelettes, steak and so on.

CINNAMON, a sweet spice made from ground tree bark; used in cakes, cookies, candies, coffee and some stews.

CLOVE, used whole, but sparingly, in pork, ham and fruit desserts.

GINGER, a bulb-like root with a pretty flower; used in cakes, cookies, candies, chutney or, ground with black pepper and salt, as a seasoning for steak.

MARJORAM, used with fish, meat, pork and in meat marinades.

MACE, the lacy outer sheath of the nutmeg kernel with a stronger nutmeg flavour.

NUTMEG, the stone of the nutmeg fruit; used in drinks, cakes, desserts and with some egg dishes and milk puddings.

PAPRIKA, made from dried sweet peppers; used in fish and meat dishes.

PARSLEY, used in sauces, fish and meat dishes and as a garnish.

SAPOTE, the brown fruit of a large tree has a rich, sweet flavour; used for preserves and sherbert or can be eaten raw.

SAGE, plentiful on many islands; used with poultry, pork and fish.

THYME, usually sold in small bunches with chives and parsley and tied with a wisp of straw; these are always called 'seasonings'.

TONKA BEAN, sometimes used instead of vanilla.

TARRAGON, used in vinegar, stews and with fish.

TURMERIC, like saffron, used to colour and flavour rice and curries.

Stuffed artichoke hearts

14

APPETIZERS, HORS D'OEUVRE AND SAVOURIES

Hors d'oeuvre, or appetizers, originated to appease the pangs of hunger suffered by guests who had come a long way. Although this idea did not originate in the West Indies, people often travel some distance to a party giving importance to the titbits and savouries offered with drinks or as the start of a dinner.

Hors d'oeuvre portions should be small, the flavour sharp, arrangements eye-catching and colourful. Canapés should be served piping hot, cold appetizers well chilled. Larger portions of some of the savouries, such as cheese and chive tartlets (page 16) make supper or light lunch dishes.

STUFFED ARTICHOKE HEARTS

Preparation time 10 minutes
To serve 6

You will need

8 oz crab meat, boned and flaked
$\frac{1}{4}$ pint (U.S. $\frac{2}{3}$ cup) mayonnaise (see page 88)
6 large cooked artichoke hearts
2 tomatoes, cut into 6 thick slices
1 lettuce heart
6 capers

Moisten crab meat with a little of the mayonnaise. Place each artichoke heart on a tomato slice and arrange on a serving dish with lettuce. Pile crab meat on top, coat with remaining mayonnaise and top with capers. Chill before serving.

CHEESE BITES

Preparation time 7 minutes
To serve 6

You will need

8 oz. cream cheese
2 teaspoons finely grated onion
2 teaspoons chopped parsley
1 teaspoon chopped chives
1 tablespoon sweet chutney, drained
salt and pepper
$1\frac{1}{2}$ oz. finely minced blanched peanuts
dash paprika

Cream the cheese with the onion, parsley, chives, chutney and seasoning until well blended. Shape into bite-sized balls and roll in chopped nuts to which paprika has been added, chill. Serve on sticks stuck into a large grapefruit.

CHEESE AND CHIVE TARTLETS

Preparation time 35 minutes, plus resting time
Cooking time 25 minutes
Oven temperature 375°F., Gas Mark 5
To serve 4

You will need

FOR THE PASTRY

6 oz plain flour
pinch salt
squeeze lemon juice
iced water
6 oz. butter

FOR THE FILLING

3 tablespoons chopped chives or spring onions
1 oz. butter
12 oz. processed cheese, finely chopped
3 egg yolks
pinch salt
pinch grated nutmeg
pinch cayenne pepper
$\frac{1}{2}$ pint (U.S. $1\frac{1}{4}$ cups) cream

FOR THE PASTRY

Sieve flour and salt and mix to a rolling consistency with lemon juice and water. Roll to an oblong shape and place the butter in the centre. Fold over the bottom section of pastry, and then the top so that the butter is covered. Seal edges, turn dough at right angles, roll out and fold in three to an envelope shape. Repeat five times, putting pastry into the refrigerator two or three times to rest. Roll out the pastry very thinly and line four large patty tins or saucers. Flute edges.

FOR THE FILLING

Fry the chives or spring onions in $\frac{1}{2}$ oz. butter until golden brown, stirring all the time. Allow to cool slightly, then stir in the processed cheese.
Beat the egg yolks with the salt, nutmeg and cayenne, add the cream and whisk with a wire or rotary whisk until well blended. Turn the cheese and chive mixture into the lined patty tins or saucers and pour the egg and cream mixture over until the tartlets are just full. Dot with the remaining butter and bake in a moderately hot oven for 25 minutes until the filling sets and browns slightly. Serve very hot.
Note
A larger baking tin can be used and the tart served sliced.

Cheese and chive tartlets

DEVILLED CHICKEN BITES

Preparation time 7 minutes
Cooking time 1 minute
To serve 6

You will need

6 oz. minced cooked chicken
1 tablespoon finely chopped parsley
1 tablespoon finely chopped chives
1 tablespoon grated onion
1 tablespoon curry powder
salt
made mustard
1 egg, beaten
2 tablespoons crisp breadcrumbs (raspings)
deep fat or oil for frying

Blend chicken with parsley, chives, onion, curry powder and salt. Bind with mustard and shape into 'bite-sized' balls. Roll in beaten egg and breadcrumbs, chill. Just before serving fry in a wire basket in hot deep fat for 1 minute. Drain and serve very hot on sticks.

VARIATIONS

Minced ham, hard cheese or pounded fish can be used instead of chicken.

Blue Mountain cocktail

BLUE MOUNTAIN COCKTAIL

Preparation time 10 minutes
To serve 4

You will need

2 grapefruit
2 oranges or ortaniques
dash Angostura bitters
sugar to taste
4 tablespoons white rum

Halve grapefruit, remove segments, discarding pith, skin and pips. Repeat with oranges or ortaniques. Mix fruit sections, sprinkle with Angostura and sugar. Pile back into grapefruit shells and pour over rum. Serve on crushed ice on individual dishes.

CUBAN DICED FISH

Preparation time 5 minutes, plus overnight marinating
To serve 4

You will need

1½ lb. tuna, skinned, boned and cut into small cubes
½ pint (U.S. 1¼ cups) strained lime juice
salt and pepper
1 onion, thinly sliced

Put fish in a deep dish with a cover, pour over lime juice and sprinkle with salt. Cover and allow to stand in the refrigerator overnight.
Drain, season to taste with pepper and mix with onion rings. Serve with French dressing (see page 89).
Note
Dolphin, fresh salmon or any solid white fish can be used in place of tuna, but tinned fish is unsuitable.

AVOCADO DIP
(Illustrated in colour on page 19)

Preparation time 5 minutes
To serve 6

You will need

1 large avocado pear
2 teaspoons lime juice
1 teaspoon grated onion
4 tablespoons mayonnaise (see page 88)
dash Tabasco sauce
pinch salt
paprika

Cut avocado in half lengthways, remove, but do not discard the stone. Scoop out flesh, mash to a paste, add remaining ingredients, except paprika and blend well. Put the stone back in the mixture to prevent discolouration and chill well. Put into serving dish and serve, sprinkled with paprika.

PLANTAIN CRISPS
(Illustrated in colour on page 19)

Preparation time 5 minutes
Cooking time 10 minutes
To serve 6

You will need

2 ripe plantains, peeled
flour and cinnamon for dusting
1 oz. butter or margarine

Slice plantains lengthways, cut into convenient-sized chips. Dust with flour and cinnamon mixture and fry quickly in hot butter or margarine until golden. Drain and serve hot or cold.

COCONUT CRISPS

(Illustrated in colour on page 19)

Preparation time 10 minutes
Cooking time 30 minutes
Oven temperature 350°F., Gas Mark 4
To serve 6

You will need

8 oz. peeled ripe coconut, grated
4 oz. plain flour
1½ teaspoons baking powder
1 oz. butter or margarine
¼ pint (U.S. ⅔ cup) milk

Toast the coconut in a moderate oven for 10 minutes, shaking to ensure even browning and drying. Allow to cool.
Sift flour and baking powder in a bowl. Heat butter or margarine in milk until it melts. Cool, then pour into flour mixture and blend. Add coconut, mixing to a smooth paste. Turn on to a floured board, roll out thinly, and cut into fingers. Place on a well greased baking sheet and bake in a moderate oven for 15-20 minutes until delicately brown. Cool and store until required.

AUBERGINE SPREAD

(Illustrated in colour on page 19)

Preparation time 5 minutes
To serve 6

You will need

1 large aubergine
1 teaspoon grated onion
½ clove garlic, crushed
1 tomato, peeled and pulped
1 teaspoon sugar
2 tablespoons vinegar
2 tablespoons olive oil

Cut one slice from aubergine. Peel remainder and cook in boiling salted water until tender. Boil or fry reserved slice. Pound aubergine, add all other ingredients and blend. If too thick, add a little more olive oil. Serve chilled, garnished with reserved slice.

FISH DIP

(Illustrated in colour on page 19)

Preparation time 5 minutes
To serve 6

You will need

2 tablespoons lime juice
4 oz. cream cheese
6 oz. cooked fish, well pounded
salt and pepper
1 tablespoon chopped chives
1 tablespoon chopped parsley
dash Tabasco sauce
2 tablespoons single cream
1 teaspoon chopped eschalots or spring onions

Beat the lime juice into the cheese. Season fish with salt and pepper, add chives and parsley and blend with beaten cheese. Add Tabasco and thin to a dipping consistency with cream. Serve chilled, sprinkled with eschalots or spring onions.

BREADFRUIT CRISPS

Preparation time 5 minutes
Cooking time 10 minutes
To serve 6

You will need

1 breadfruit, parboiled and peeled
salt
3 tablespoons oil

Remove breadfruit core, cut into ½-inch slices and drop these into salted water. Drain, dry and fry in hot oil until golden. Drain and sprinkle with salt. Serve hot or cold.

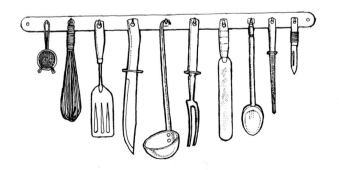

Plantain crisps, fish dip, aubergine spread, coconut crisps and avocado dip

Grapefruit consommé

SOUPS

Nothing is more refreshing and reviving in a hot climate than a really good cold soup, yet hot peppery soups, the pepperpots, are standard fare throughout the Caribbean. Cold soups are often quick and easy to make, especially in a blender and most of the cold soups in this chapter can also be served hot.

One tends to think the Caribbean nights are always languorous, but Trade Winds sometimes come with a cool nip and in high mountain districts in Jamaica,

Trinidad, Puerto Rico and the Dominican Republic (not to be confused with Dominica, which is also mountainous) hot soups are called for.

In the Bahamas fish or conch chowder is almost the standard Sunday lunch, like the roast beef of England, but a very good fish soup can be made without conch (pronounced 'conk'). In Jamaica, fish soup is 'Fish Tea' and sometimes called 'Strong Back', but this term is applied to anything nourishing 'make strong back'.

A BASIC STOCK

Preparation time 10 minutes
Cooking time 4 hours
To make 4 pints (U.S. 10 cups) stock

You will need

3 onions
2 cloves
3 lb. lean stewing beef
8 oz. beef bones
3 carrots
2 sticks celery
2 root vegetables as available, tannia and eddoe, in the Caribbean, parsnip and turnip in Europe
clove garlic
bouquet garni (2 sprigs thyme, 1 sprig marjoram, 1 bay leaf, 1 sprig parsley, 2 chives or 1 spring onion)
1 teaspoon salt
1 teaspoon pepper
8 pints (U.S. 5 quarts) water

Stick one onion with the cloves. Put all ingredients into a large saucepan, all whole and uncut, except for scraping the root vegetables. Bring water to the boil and skim several times before turning down the heat and simmering for 4 hours. Cool, remove fat and strain. The meat and vegetables can be eaten as a simple meal or used for other recipes.
Note
Chicken, turkey, ham bone or fish stock is prepared in the same manner.

Tinned consommé and beef stock are not always available in remote districts and in any case, the home-made variety is better and more nourishing. Meat, bones, poultry skins and giblets, bacon rind and scraps of vegetables, should be wrapped in plastic bags or airtight containers and can be kept for a few days in the refrigerator.

Peanut butter cream soup with foo foo

Callaloo soup

PEANUT BUTTER CREAM SOUP

Peanuts were brought to Surinam from Indonesia in 1890 when the Javanese landed. One finds peanut butter in much of the cooking in Surinam today and as chicken is a basic food, the two were combined in this soup. No salt is used in accordance with East Indian cooking procedure.

Preparation time 5 minutes
Cooking time   15 minutes
To serve   4 – 6

You will need

2 oz. butter
2 oz. flour
3 pints (U.S. $7\frac{1}{2}$ cups) chicken stock (see page 21)
12 oz. peanut butter
pepper

TO GARNISH
4 tablespoons finely chopped cooked chicken
1 tablespoon finely chopped parsley

Melt butter in a saucepan, stir in flour and cook for 2 minutes. Reserve 1 pint (U.S. $2\frac{1}{2}$ cups) stock and slowly stir remainder into the flour mixture and bring to the boil. Blend remaining stock with peanut butter and when quite smooth, add this to soup. Season with pepper to taste and simmer for a further 10 minutes. Serve very hot topped with chopped chicken and parsley. Serve with Foo Foo (see page 144).

CALLALOO SOUP

Preparation time 15 minutes
Cooking time $1\frac{1}{2}$ hours
To serve   4

You will need

4 oz. lean bacon or salt pork
generous $\frac{3}{4}$ pint (U.S. 2 cups) water
salt and pepper
2 crabs
1 lb. callaloo leaves
sprig thyme
2 chives
sprig parsley
8 okras, chopped
1 onion, sliced
1 clove garlic, crushed
$\frac{1}{2}$ oz. butter

Remove rind or skin and cut bacon into strips or pork into chunks. Put into a thick saucepan with water, salt and pepper. Bring to boil and simmer for 1 hour. Scrub crabs and scald in boiling water. Remove veins from callaloo and chop with stalks. Tie herbs together. Add all other ingredients, except butter, to the bacon or pork and simmer for a further 30 minutes. Remove crabs, take out meat and return to soup, reserving claws. Stir butter into soup and serve garnished with crabs' claws.
Note
Dumplings are sometimes served with this soup to make it even more of a meal.

CALYPSO CUCUMBER CREAM SOUP

Preparation time 7 minutes
Cooking time 35 minutes
To serve 4

You will need

3 – 4 cucumbers, according to size
1 oz. butter
1 oz. flour
1 pint (U.S. 2½ cups) chicken stock
½ pint (U.S. 1¼ cups) milk
1 onion, thinly sliced
¼ pint (U.S. ⅔ cup) single cream
salt and pepper
1 tablespoon chopped chives

Peel cucumbers, cut into slices and remove the seeds. Melt the butter and cook cucumbers for 10 minutes over a low heat. Stir in the flour and add chicken stock slowly, stirring all the time. Heat the milk with the onion rings to boiling point and add to cucumber mixture, still stirring. Simmer over a low heat for 10 minutes. Sieve, stir in half the cream and season to taste. Turn into individual bowls or dishes and chill thoroughly. Swirl in cream just before serving and sprinkle with chives.
Note
West Indian cucumbers look different from the shiny, long green European type. They are short and stubby, and dark green or yellow skinned. However, the flavour is good and when very ripe, they pulp easily. When using European cucumbers, two should be enough for four servings.

Calypso cucumber cream soup

CHILLED AVOCADO CREAM SOUP

Preparation time 10 minutes
To serve 4

You will need

3 small or 2 large green peppers, de-seeded and chopped
2 eschalots or spring onions, chopped
2 large, very ripe avocado pears
1 tablespoon strained lime juice
2 teaspoons salt
1 pint (U.S. 2½ cups) milk
4 tablespoons cream
paprika

Pound peppers and eschalots or spring onions, in a pestle and mortar or put into a blender. Scoop flesh from avocados, retaining the stones and mash. Blend avocado pulp with pepper and eschalot mixture, add lime juice and salt and then, very slowly, add milk, beating all the time. Replace stones in mixture to prevent discolouration and chill well. Serve with a spoonful of cream and sprinkling of paprika on top of each portion.

GRAPEFRUIT CONSOMME
(Illustrated in colour on page 20)

Preparation time 10 minutes
To serve 4

You will need

¾ pint (U.S. 2 cups) strained grapefruit juice
2 tablespoons strained orange juice
2 tablespoons strained lime juice
dash Angostura Bitters
2 or 3 grapefruit, according to size
1 packet lemon jelly
scant ¼ pint (U.S. ½ cup) boiling water
mint or parsley

Blend juices and Angostura in a jug. Peel grapefruit, divide into segments, removing all pith and pips and chop. Dissolve jelly in water, allow to cool slightly then add to fruit juice mixture. Pour into individual bowls or dishes and stir in segments. Chill thoroughly and serve topped with mint or parsley.

Fish chowder

Add the fish, cut into small pieces and simmer for a further 15 minutes. Season with salt and pepper to taste and serve in a big tureen. Serve with French bread, toasted if liked.
Note
Some cooks make a paste of 1 teaspoon cornflour mixed with 2 tablespoons dry sherry; added to the soup just before serving it gives slightly more body. Where conch are available, reduce the amount of fish and add conch meat.

FISH TEA or 'STRONG BACK'

Tourists in my local fishmarket often reject the fish head with a shudder but local people pounce on it, knowing the tasty and nourishing 'tea' it will make.

Preparation time 15 minutes
Cooking time   45 – 50 minutes
To serve   4 – 5

You will need

2 teaspoons chopped thyme
2 teaspoons chopped parsley
2 teaspoons chopped chives
1 oz. butter
1 large fish head, such as dolphin, cleaned
2 pints (U.S. 5 cups) water
1½ teaspoons salt
1 onion, chopped
3 medium-sized English potatoes, peeled and diced
2 cloves
¼ teaspoon pepper

TO GARNISH
1 teaspoon chopped chives
1 teaspoon chopped parsley

Fry chopped herbs in butter without allowing them to brown. Add the fish head, water and salt and bring to the boil in a large saucepan. Skim, add vegetables, cloves and pepper and simmer for 35-40 minutes until all the vegetables are soft. Remove the fish head, skin and bone it, flake the flesh and return to the soup. Serve sprinkled with chives and parsley.
Note
For a thicker soup, blend 1 oz. flour and 4 tablespoons milk to a paste, add to the soup and simmer for a further 5 minutes.

FISH CHOWDER

Preparation time 15 minutes
Cooking time   2½ hours
To serve   4 – 6

You will need

1 cooked crayfish or small lobster
2 cooked crabs (or can crab meat)
12 cooked prawns
12 oz. filleted white fish, reserve skin, head and bones
3 pints (U.S. 7½ cups) water
2 tablespoons olive oil
2 onions, chopped
2 tomatoes, skinned and sliced
1 carrot, peeled and diced
1 small green pepper, de-seeded and chopped
1 clove garlic, crushed
1 bay leaf, chopped
sprig thyme
sprig parsley
2 chives
½ teaspoon saffron powder
salt and pepper

Remove shell fish from shells, put these with skin, heads and bones from filleted white fish in the water. Boil for 1 hour, strain. Heat the oil, gently fry vegetables, herbs, tied together, saffron and seasoning without browning. Have fish stock boiling (if it is not boiling fast the oil will not mix) add the fried vegetables, herbs and seasonings and simmer for about 45 minutes or until vegetables are very tender.

SUNSHINE SOUP

Preparation time 7 minutes
Cooking time 50 minutes
To serve 4

You will need

2 lb. pumpkin
salt
1 large onion, finely chopped
2 tomatoes, sliced
2 teaspoons chopped chives
sprig parsley
$\frac{1}{4}$ pint (U.S. $\frac{2}{3}$ cup) chicken stock (see page 21)
paprika
$\frac{1}{4}$ pint (U.S. $\frac{2}{3}$ cup) single cream

Cut the pumpkin into four big pieces and cook in boiling salted water for 15 minutes. Drain, scoop the flesh from the skin. Put the pumpkin and all the other vegetables, half the chives and the parsley with the chicken stock in a saucepan. Bring to the boil, lower the heat and simmer very gently for 35 minutes with the lid on the saucepan. Allow to cool slightly, strain and sieve (if too much stock remains, pour off some of the liquid). Allow the purée to become almost cold, then season with paprika and a very little salt. Stir in half the cream. Mix well, pour into serving bowl and refrigerate until fairly thick and firm. Swirl in the remaining cream just before serving and sprinkle with remaining chives.

FLOATS

Preparation time 7 minutes
Cooking time 15 minutes
To serve 4 – 6

You will need

1 egg
1 tablespoon water
$\frac{1}{2}$ teaspoon salt
pinch paprika
pinch curry powder or cayenne pepper
1 teaspoon baking powder
1 oz. flour
large knob butter, melted

Beat the egg lightly with the water, salt, paprika and curry powder or cayenne. Sift the baking powder into the flour. Add butter alternately with the flour to the egg and water, beating all the time. Drop the mixture from the tip of a spoon into boiling soup, cover and simmer for 15 minutes.
Note
A little chopped parsley or saffron may be used to give colour if the soup is pale.

DUMPLINGS

In the West Indies, dumplings and floats are popular as are all such dough additions. The G is usually dropped and dumplings are known as *dumplins*.

Preparation time 7 minutes
Cooking time 10 – 15 minutes
To serve 4 – 6

You will need

4 oz. plain flour
1 teaspoon baking powder
$\frac{1}{4}$ teaspoon salt
large pinch grated nutmeg
knob butter
1 egg yolk
3 tablespoons milk

Sift the flour with the baking powder, salt and nutmeg. Cut in the butter with a knife until the mixture looks like coarse crumbs. Beat the egg yolk with the milk and add to the flour mixture quickly without beating. Drop this dough by the spoonful into boiling soup or salted water. Cover and cook for 10-15 minutes according to the size of the dumplings. Drain before serving.

VARIATIONS

Chopped chives, parsley or grated Parmesan cheese may be added, or for more substantial dumplings, add chopped chicken liver.

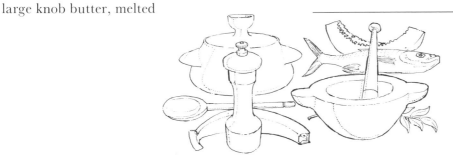

Avocado sauce, peanut sauce, hunter's orange sauce, Creole sauce.

SAUCES, MARINADES AND BUTTERS

Sauce, in the islands, must be approached with some caution; call for pepper and what comes will be pepper sauce without which no West Indian really relishes his food. One of my closest friends in Grenada, who travels a lot, carries with her a handbag-size plastic bottle of her beloved pepper sauce; she is quite unable to eat without it! If ground pepper is wanted, ask for *black* pepper. Tabasco may seem fiery to European palates but it pales to a mild ketchup besides the genuine hot sauce, guaranteed, as one ex-patriot told me, to 'blow up a bank or a post office'.

Meat and poultry is frequently rather tough, in the Caribbean and is improved by marinating for a few hours or overnight, as is all meat, especially any that has been frozen. Well flavoured savoury butters are excellent served with meat, fish and vegetables, for cooking, and for sandwich fillings.

BROWN SAUCE

Preparation time 5 minutes
Cooking time 10 minutes
To serve 4

You will need

1 oz. butter
1 oz. flour
½ pint (U.S. 1¼ cups) beef stock (see page 21)
salt and pepper

Melt the butter and stir in the flour to make a smooth paste. Continue stirring until the paste is light brown. Remove from heat and add the stock, stirring all the time. Return to the heat and bring to the boil, stirring continuously and boil for 2 minutes. Season to taste. More liquid can be added to make a thinner sauce.

VARIATIONS
The following may be added to the basic brown sauce:

1. 4 oz. diced cooked pork, ½ teaspoon chopped thyme and 2 teaspoons each chopped cooked carrot and onion.
2. 2 tablespoons cooked green peas, 1 tablespoon chopped cooked onion, 1 tablespoon capers and 2 tablespoons white rum.
3. 2 teaspoons chopped chives, 6 ground peppercorns, 3 tablespoons vinegar, 1 teaspoon chopped parsley, 1 teaspoon Worcestershire sauce and ¼ teaspoon made mustard.
4. 1 teaspoon chopped eschalots or spring onions, 2 skinned and chopped cooked tomatoes and 3 tablespoons rum.
5. 3 sieved cooked chicken livers, 1 tablespoon guava or red currant jelly, 1 teaspoon grated orange rind and a dash of Tabasco sauce.
6. Use fish stock in place of beef and add a pinch each powdered thyme, marjoram and sage, 1 teaspoon finely chopped chives, pinch grated nutmeg and the juice of 1 lime.

WHITE SAUCE

Preparation time 3 minutes
Cooking time 7 minutes
To serve 4

You will need

1 oz. butter or margarine
1 oz. flour
½ pint (U.S. 1¼ cups) milk
salt and pepper

Melt the butter in a saucepan, stir in the flour to a smooth paste and cook for 1 minute. Remove from heat and slowly add milk stirring all the time. Bring to the boil, stirring continuously and boil for 2 minutes. Season to taste.

VARIATIONS

The following may be added to the basic white sauce:
1. 2 finely chopped hard-boiled eggs and a teaspoon of parsley.
2. 3 oz. grated cheese and 2 egg yolks.
3. 1 tablespoon chopped chives, tarragon, callaloo or watercress.

WEST INDIAN SAUCE

Preparation time 10 minutes, plus 10 minutes marinating
Cooking time 20 – 25 minutes
To serve 4 – 6

You will need

1 pint (U.S. 2½ cups) shrimps or prawns
salt
strained juice 2 limes
4 oz. butter
1 onion, chopped
2 small tomatoes, skinned and very thinly sliced
2 tablespoons chopped parsley
2 cloves garlic, crushed
¼ teaspoon pepper
2 teaspoons celery salt
½ pint (U.S. 1¼ cups) chicken or fish stock (see page 21)
2 eggs
2 tablespoons vinegar

West Indian sauce

Scald shrimps or prawns in boiling salted water, peel off heads and shells and soak in lime juice for 10 minutes. Meanwhile, heat butter in a saucepan, fry onion, tomatoes, parsley and garlic until golden and season with pepper and celery salt. Continue frying until almost all the butter is absorbed, then pour on the stock and bring to the boil, stirring all the time. Drain shrimps or prawns, add them to the sauce and continue cooking over a very low heat for 15 minutes or until fish is soft. Beat the eggs, blend with the vinegar and stir into the sauce just before serving; do not allow to boil. Serve very hot, with boiled rice, eggs or plain poached fish.
Note
This may seem more of a meal than a sauce. With the addition of chutney, almost any white fish becomes interesting when served with rice and masked with West Indian sauce.

PEANUT SAUCE

Preparation time 4 minutes
Cooking time 10 minutes
To serve 4 – 6

You will need

2 tablespoons grated onion
2 tablespoons olive oil
1 oz. dark brown sugar
1 tablespoon lime juice
2 tablespoons peanut butter
½ pint (U.S. 1¼ cups) coconut milk
salt

Lightly fry the onion in the heated oil for 5 minutes. Add the sugar, lime juice and peanut butter, blending thoroughly. Slowly add the coconut milk, stirring all the time. Season with salt and continue cooking over a gentle heat until the sauce thickens.

CREOLE SAUCE

Preparation time 10 minutes
Cooking time 45 minutes
To serve 4

You will need

1 oz. butter
1 onion, chopped
½ teaspoon curry powder
½ oz. flour
1 pint (U.S. 2½ cups) beef or chicken stock (see page 21)
1 thin slice ham
1 tablespoon mango chutney (see page 111) or any sweet chutney
1 small green pawpaw, peeled and chopped
salt
1 teaspoon lime juice
4 tablespoons single cream

Melt the butter in a saucepan and fry the onion in this until golden brown. Add the curry powder and flour to make a paste and cook for 5 minutes without browning. Slowly stir in the stock and bring to the boil before adding the remaining ingredients, except the lime juice and cream. Cook over a low heat for 40 minutes stirring from time to time. Cool slightly, sieve and season to taste. Bring once more to the boil, add the lime juice and stir in the cream.
Note
Made with fish stock, this sauce is suitable for use with shellfish. Apple can be substituted for pawpaw.

HUNTER'S ORANGE SAUCE

On many Caribbean and Bahama islands there is rough shooting and on nearly all, oranges are plentiful.

Preparation time 3 minutes
Cooking time 7 minutes
To serve 4 – 6

You will need

1 oz. flour
5 tablespoons water
2 tablespoons fat from the pan in which a bird has been roasted or bacon fat
salt and pepper
pinch cayenne pepper
¼ pint (U.S. ⅔ cup) strained orange juice
4 teaspoons finely grated orange rind
1 tablespoon guava jelly (see page 113)
½ oz. butter
1 tablespoon rum

Mix the flour and water to a smooth paste and add the fat, stirring all the time. Season with salt, pepper and cayenne, add the orange juice and most of the rind. Still stirring, simmer over a low heat for 5 minutes. Add guava jelly, butter and rum just before serving and cook until the jelly melts. Serve sprinkled with remaining orange rind.
Note
If guava jelly is not available, use any jam or jelly that is fairly sharp, such as red currant jelly. I have made this sauce successfully with a spoonful of honey.

BARBADOS BROWN SUGAR SAUCE

Preparation time 3 minutes
Cooking time 4 – 5 minutes
To serve 4 – 6

You will need

4 tablespoons very dark brown sugar
2 oz. butter
1 egg, lightly beaten
4 tablespoons rum
pinch grated nutmeg

Beat the sugar and butter together to a soft cream. Beat in the egg and rum and stir over a very low heat until all the ingredients are well blended. Add nutmeg just before serving.
Note
This sauce is good with baked bananas, rice pudding, cereals, plain ice cream and milk pudding. It is a great favourite with children if the rum is omitted.

Preparation of coconut cream

COCONUT CREAM

Preparation time 15 minutes
To serve   4 – 6

You will need

1 coconut

To prepare the coconut, pierce the three eyes at one end. Empty out the milk and strain it. Put the nut eye end down on a hard surface, give it a sharp bang and it will break into convenient size pieces. Scoop the flesh from the shell (the brown skin can be left on) and grind or flake it (a mincing machine or coffee grinder can be used for this). Blend thoroughly with the milk and pour into a cheese cloth or piece of muslin. Squeeze the cream out through the cloth or muslin and repeat this several times to extract it all.
Note
Desiccated coconut can be used by soaking it for 1 hour in hot water and squeezing as before. It makes a much thinner cream than fresh coconut.

MARINADE FOR MEAT, POULTRY OR FISH

Meat in the Caribbean is apt to be tough from long freezing and personally I find marinating essential. Where available, and this applies to nearly all places in the West Indies, I add pawpaw seeds to the above and wrap the meat in pawpaw skins or leaves for about 1 hour before marinating. Do not, however, let it stand longer or the pepsin in the pawpaw 'digests' the meat and makes it soft and tasteless.

Preparation time 3 minutes
To make   ¼ pint

You will need

2 tablespoons vinegar (or lime juice for fish)
2 tablespoons olive oil
2 tablespoons rum
1½ teaspoons salt
1½ teaspoons sugar (omit for fish)
1 onion, chopped
1 clove garlic, crushed
½ small chilli, chopped or 1 teaspoon black pepper
1 teaspoon chopped marjoram (or thyme for poultry and fish)

Blend all the ingredients, put into a deep platter, such as a soup plate and allow the food to stand in the marinade. Allow 30 minutes on each side for meat and poultry and 5 minutes for fish.
Note
Use the marinade for basting, adding 1 tablespoon flour and ½ oz. butter to this when mixed with the meat, poultry or fish juices. This makes a good sauce to serve with the food.

QUICK MARINADE TO STORE

Preparation time 5 minutes
Cooking time   2 – 3 minutes
To make   1 pint

You will need

1 pint (U.S. 2½ cups) olive oil
1 clove garlic, cut
12 peppercorns
1 sprig thyme, marjoram or rosemary, stripped
2 limes

Blend all the ingredients except the limes, put in a saucepan and heat, but do not boil. Strain and stand the meat in the mixture or, in the case of chops, paint it on thickly. Squeeze the limes over the food and mixture and allow to stand for 1 hour.
Note
The above quantity is enough to bottle and store, halve the quantities if it is to be used at once. The lime juice is added at the time of use. This is a meat marinade, unsuitable for fish.

Herb butter

for serving, cut into $\frac{1}{4}$-inch slices and use with grilled meat, poultry or fish or with vegetables.

1. Wash and fillet 4 anchovies, pound, sieve and add to the butter.
2. Boil 2 teaspoons chopped chives for 2 minutes. Drain, crush and add to the butter.
3. Add $\frac{1}{2}$ teaspoon curry powder and a squeeze of lime to the butter.
4. Add 1 very finely chopped clove garlic to the butter.
5. Pound 4 oz. cooked lobster, prawns or shrimps and add to the butter.
6. Add $\frac{1}{2}$ teaspoon chopped parsley, a squeeze of lime and a pinch of salt and pepper to the butter.
7. Cook 2 tomatoes, sieve and add to the butter with a pinch of salt.
8. Add 2 drops Tabasco sauce to the butter.

HERB BUTTER

Preparation time 5 minutes
Cooking time 5 minutes
To serve 4

You will need

1 teaspoon chopped chives
2 teaspoons chopped parsley
1 teaspoon chopped tarragon
$4\frac{1}{2}$ tablespoons hot water
2 oz. butter
salt and pepper

Boil the chives, parsley and tarragon in water for 5 minutes. Strain the herbs and blend with the butter. Season to taste.

VARIATION

For green herb butter, add a shredded spinach or callaloo leaf, to the boiling herbs.

SAVOURY BUTTERS

Using 2 oz. butter, any of the following savoury butters can be made. When thoroughly mixed make a small roll, about 1-inch in diameter, wrap in wet greaseproof paper and chill. When hard and ready

CLARIFIED BUTTER

Preparation time 3 – 5 minutes
To serve 4

You will need

2 oz. butter

Stand the butter in a cup in a basin of hot water. When melted, pour off the oiled butter and discard the sediment.
Note
This is the fat used most often in Indian recipes and is called *ghee*.

BLACK BUTTER

Preparation time 2 minutes
Cooking time 5 – 7 minutes
To serve 4

You will need

2 oz. butter
black pepper

Melt the butter and heat until dark brown. Season with pepper to taste.

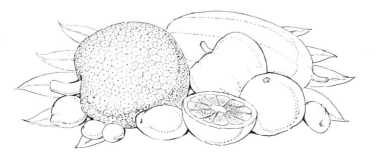

RICE DISHES AND CURRIES

Brought to the Caribbean by East Indians, rice today is the principal food of the islanders. They eat it with okra, with pigs' tails and above all with peas, which are in fact *red beans* in Jamaica. 'Peas and Rice' (see page 143) is cooked on every island, down from the Bahamas, where it is known as Hoppin' John, to the South American mainland. Methods of cooking rice are as numerous as the different types, almost every plantation producing a slightly different strain. The peoples of the Caribbean all have their chosen way of preparation. Some follow the European custom of washing and boiling until the liquid is absorbed; others use Creole baked rice; the Chinese cook in a special metal rice pot; Dutch islanders wash and wash until the water is crystal clear before simmering their rice; Lebanese cook in butter; Indonesians have their 'rice table' and so it goes on. Cooking methods might fill a complete book, but not all are palatable to non-West

Indians, so I have chosen a few of the more attractive and original ways of using rice. Chicken, fish or cheese and rice loaf, for instance, would be useful anywhere, West Indian Rice Pie is a change from the usual shepherd's pie, and Rum Rice Fritters are easy to make and could grace any meal.

As in all hot places, curries are often eaten, the hotter the better for West Indians. People unused to eating curry cannot understand why such spicy food should be cooked in the tropics, but spice has a definite antiseptic value and true curries are never made with left-over, bacteria-carrying food. They cool because they cause perspiration, but eaten in excess they can produce prickly heat. The fat used should be *ghee* (see page 31), butter or olive oil, and coconut, peanut and tamarind provide useful flavourings.

In this chapter, recipes are somewhat modified for general consumption.

SAFFRON RICE

Preparation time 5 minutes
Cooking time 25 – 30 minutes
To serve 4

You will need

1 onion, finely chopped
3 tablespoons olive oil
8 oz. rice
pinch saffron powder
salt
1 pint (U.S. 2½ cups) boiling chicken stock (see page 21)

Fry the onion in the heated oil until soft but not brown. Add the rice, saffron and salt and stir to colour the rice evenly. Add stock and cook over a low heat for 15 – 20 minutes, stirring occasionally. Turn off the heat and leave rice on the warm stove for a minute to absorb the remainder of the stock, if any.

Note
This dish is not served alone, it is an accompaniment to other dishes or the basis of certain rice recipes.

Rice loaf

RICE LOAF

Preparation time 7 minutes
Cooking time about 1 hour 10 minutes
Oven temperature 350 – 375°F., Gas Mark 4 – 5
To serve 4 – 6

You will need

1 lb. rice
2 pints (U.S. 5 cups) boiling beef, chicken or fish stock (see page 21)
8 oz. finely minced cooked meat, chicken or fish
1 small onion, chopped
4 oz. left-over vegetables, such as cooked peas, a few mushrooms or cooked carrot, cut in small dice
1 tablespoon strained lime juice
2 tablespoons chopped parsley
dash Tabasco sauce
pinch grated nutmeg
½ pint (U.S. 1¼ cups) thick white sauce (see page 28) for chicken or fish, brown or West Indian sauce (see pages 27 and 28) for meat
salt and pepper

TO GARNISH
grilled tomato slices

Prepare the rice by washing several times, draining and adding to the fast boiling stock. Cook over a medium heat for 30 minutes until tender.
While the rice is cooking, blend the minced meat,

chicken or fish with the onion and other vegetables, lime juice, parsley, Tabasco, nutmeg and sauce. Season to taste. Drain the rice well and line a buttered loaf tin with half the rice, well packed into the corners. Pile in the filling and finish with a thick firm layer of cooked rice. Cover with buttered foil or greaseproof paper and bake in a moderate to moderately hot oven for 40–45 minutes. Turn out with care and garnish with grilled tomato slices.

COLD SCRAMBLED EGGS AND RICE

Preparation time 7 minutes
Cooking time 5 minutes
To serve 4

You will need

8 oz. cooked rice
2 teaspoons brown sugar
pinch salt
pinch curry powder
4 oz. cooked peas
4 oz. cooked carrots, finely diced
4 oz. cooked okra, thinly sliced (optional)
3 eggs
2 tablespoons milk
1 oz. butter
pepper

TO GARNISH
lettuce

While the rice is still hot, pat it on to a dish to form a bed. Mix the sugar, salt and curry powder together, sprinkle on to the rice, and arrange the well mixed vegetables all round the dish. Scramble the eggs with the milk and butter, season to taste with salt and pepper and pile on top of the rice
Cover, put in the coolest possible place to get cold, but do not refrigerate. Garnish with crisp lettuce.
Note
This dish can also be served hot, but is a very useful light lunch dish, easily served outside in the heat of the day.
The same arrangement of cold rice and vegetables can be made with shrimps, lobster or left-over minced cold chicken instead of eggs.

PINEAPPLE CHICKEN WITH SAFFRON RICE

(Illustrated in colour on page 37)

Preparation time 15 minutes, plus 1 hour
            marinating
Cooking time 40 – 45 minutes
To serve 4 – 6

You will need

1 medium-sized chicken, cut into joints
salt
4 tablespoons strained lime juice
4 tablespoons oil
2 tablespoons stoned raisins
2 tablespoons rum
dash Tabasco sauce
2 cooked tomatoes, skinned and pulped
$\frac{1}{4}$ teaspoon pepper
1 oz. butter
$\frac{1}{2}$ pineapple, peeled and cut into cubes
soft breadcrumbs
8 – 12 oz. (weight before cooking) saffron rice
    (see page 32)
1 orange, thinly sliced

Rub the chicken pieces with salt and marinate in
lime juice for 1 hour. Heat the oil and fry the
chicken quickly until browned. Reduce heat and
cook for a further 10 minutes. Add the raisins, rum,
Tabasco and pulped tomatoes, season with salt
and pepper and stir. Cover and cook for a further
15-20 minutes over a low heat.
While the chicken is cooking, melt the butter, roll
the pineapple cubes in breadcrumbs and fry to a
delicate brown. Put the hot saffron rice on to a
large dish and flatten it to form a bed. Pile the
chicken on to the rice and pour over the sauce. Top
with the pineapple cubes and garnish with orange
slices.

WEST INDIAN RICE PIE

Preparation time 7 minutes
Cooking time 1 hour
Oven temperature 375°F., Gas Mark 5
To serve 4 – 5

You will need

1 lb. minced raw beef, or mixed beef and pork
1 onion, finely minced
$\frac{1}{2}$ teaspoon chopped thyme
$\frac{1}{2}$ teaspoon chopped parsley
$\frac{1}{2}$ clove garlic, minced
1 tablespoon Worcestershire sauce
1 pint (U.S. $2\frac{1}{2}$ cups) beef stock (see page 21) or
    canned consommé
$\frac{1}{2}$ oz. butter
1 lb. cooked rice
salt and pepper
$\frac{1}{2}$ oz. crisp breadcrumbs (raspings)
paprika

Brown the minced meat in its own fat, add the
onion, thyme, parsley and garlic. Blend with the
Worcestershire sauce and a little of the stock and
simmer for 15 minutes. In a buttered pie dish, put
half the cooked rice, cover with the meat mixture,
season to taste and add the rest of the stock. Cover
with remaining rice, sprinkle with breadcrumbs
and paprika, dot with butter and bake in a moderately hot oven for 40 minutes.
Serve with brown sauce (see page 27) if liked.
Note
This is really the rice version of Shepherd's Pie;
one is more likely to have cooked rice than English
potatoes on hand in the islands. The same basis
can be used with cooked fish, using fish stock and
one or two drops of Tabasco sauce and lime juice
instead of Worcestershire sauce.

POACHED EGGS WITH RICE AND BANANAS

This makes a good breakfast or supper dish.
Breakfast on some of the islands is actually an 11.30
morning meal, people having gone to work before
8 a.m. with just a cup of tea or coffee. The lunch-
time, or breakfast break is from 11.30 – 12.30 and
work finishes at 4 p.m. A more substantial meal is
then served at around 6.30 in the evening. Darkness
always falls at about 6 – 6.30 in the tropics, the
sudden, velvety night varies very little in time and
there are no long light evenings as in European
summers.

Preparation time 10 – 15 minutes
Cooking time 35 – 40 minutes
To serve 4

You will need

8 oz. rice
4 oz. butter
$\frac{1}{2}$ stick cinnamon
2 blades mace
6 cloves
1 clove garlic, halved
1 pint (U.S. 2$\frac{1}{2}$ cups) boiling stock (see page 21)
2 onions, thinly sliced
4 medium-sized bananas, peeled and sliced
    lengthwise
4 eggs
pinch salt and pepper

Wash the rice in cold water and allow to soak for 10 minutes. While the rice soaks, heat two-thirds of the butter in a deep saucepan, add the cinnamon, mace, cloves and garlic. Drain the rice and stir into the heated butter, herbs and flavourings. Cover the rice with stock, put a clean cloth over the saucepan and put on the lid. Simmer over a low heat for 25–30 minutes. While the rice is cooking, heat remaining butter and fry onion rings and banana slices until golden brown. Set the saucepan of rice on the side of the stove for the last drops of stock to be absorbed and for the rice to dry. Poach the eggs, sprinkle with a very little salt and pepper. Turn rice on to a heated dish and remove spices and flavourings. Surround with fried onion and banana and put poached eggs on to the bed of rice.

Wash the rice and cook it in the milk, with 1$\frac{1}{2}$ oz. sugar and vanilla, for 20 minutes, or until tender. Set aside to cool. Meanwhile beat egg yolks with the rum, drain the rice if any milk is unabsorbed, and beat the egg and rum mixture into the rice. Grease a pastry board with butter, dredge with flour and spread the rice and egg mixture on to the board, about $\frac{1}{2}$-inch thick. Put in the refrigerator to chill for 15 minutes. When chilled, cut into fingers, about $\frac{3}{4}$-inch wide and 3-inches long.
Beat the whole egg and use to brush the fingers, coat with breadcrumbs. Heat the oil or fat and fry the fingers until golden brown, about 3 minutes. Sprinkle with the remaining sugar and grated coconut.

VARIATIONS
FRUIT RICE FRITTERS

Use the same method as above, mixing the rice with pulped fruit. Ripe mangoes or bananas or canned or cooked fruit, such as peaches or apricots, may be used. Sometimes I serve a sweet sauce or coconut cream (see page 30) with fruit fritters or, if the fruit is suitable, I heat a tablespoon of rum, set it alight, burn out the alcohol and pour it over the fritters.

SAVOURY FRITTERS

Cook rice in salted water and omit sugar, vanilla essence and rum. A teaspoon of mixed herbs, salt and pepper and a grated onion mixed with the beaten egg yolks, make sufficient flavouring, but curry powder or Tabasco can also be used.

RUM RICE FRITTERS

Preparation time	10 minutes, plus 15 minutes chilling time
Cooking time	25 minutes
To serve	4 – 5

You will need

6 oz. rice
1 pint (U.S. 2$\frac{1}{2}$ cups) milk
2 oz. brown sugar
$\frac{1}{2}$ teaspoon vanilla essence
2 egg yolks
4 tablespoons rum
1 whole egg
crisp breadcrumbs (raspings)
deep fat or oil for frying
grated ripe coconut

Rum rice fritters

BOILED RICE WITH COCONUT AND RAISINS

Preparation time 5 minutes
Cooking time 30 – 35 minutes
To serve 4 – 5

You will need

6 oz. rice
1 pint (U.S. 2½ cups) boiling water
pinch salt
4 oz. dark brown sugar
4 oz. butter
4 oz. stoned raisins
4 oz. peeled ripe coconut, grated

Cook the rice in the water with salt for 20 minutes, or until nearly tender. Add the sugar, stirring until it dissolves. Melt the butter, fry the raisins and coconut until the raisins are plump and the coconut golden, then stir into the rice and sugar with the melted butter left in the frying pan. Cook for 3 minutes more, stirring all the time.

VARIATIONS

This rice dish can be made with chopped nuts in place of coconut. There are many variations, sometimes I soak the raisins in rum for 10 minutes and add the rum to the melted butter, sometimes I chop a ripe banana and add this to the mixture.

MANGO RICE PUDDING

Preparation time 7 minutes
Cooking time 50 minutes
Oven temperature 375°F., Gas Mark 5
To serve 4 – 5

You will need

2 egg yolks
½ pint (U.S. 1¼ cups) milk
1 tablespoon cornflour
1½ oz. castor sugar
pinch salt
2 drops vanilla essence
¼ pint (U.S. ⅔ cup) single cream
1½ lb. cooked rice
2 large or 3 small ripe mangoes
1 oz. soft breadcrumbs

Beat egg yolks into the milk. Blend with cornflour, sugar and salt. Cook in the top of a double saucepan until the mixture thickens, about 10 minutes, stirring all the time. Remove from the heat, and stir in vanilla, cream and rice. Peel, stone and thinly slice mangoes (the early stringy type are not suitable but they need not be the very large and luscious Julies). Butter a pudding basin or pie dish and sprinkle the bottom liberally with half the breadcrumbs. Put in half the rice mixture, then well drained mango slices, reserving a few for decorating. Cover with remaining rice, sprinkle with breadcrumbs and cover with buttered greaseproof paper or foil. Bake in a moderately hot oven for 40 minutes. Set pudding aside for 10 minutes before turning out. Decorate with reserved mango slices and serve with coconut cream (see page 30) or single cream.
Note
Any suitable fresh or canned fruit may be used in place of mangoes such as apricots, peaches or pears.

RICE SOUFFLE

Preparation time 10 minutes
Cooking time 1½ hours
Oven temperature 275 – 300°F., Gas Mark 1 – 2
To serve 4 – 5

You will need

6 oz. rice
2 pints (U.S. 5 cups) boiling water
pinch salt
2 eggs, separated
grated rind and strained juice 1 or 2 limes,
    depending on size
5 oz. castor sugar
1 pint (U.S. 2½ cups) milk

Cook rice in boiling salted water for 20 minutes, until almost tender. Beat egg yolks with grated lime rind and juice. Beat in 4 oz. of the sugar and blend beaten yolk mixture with milk. Drain rice and stir egg mixture into cooked rice. Beat egg whites until stiff and gradually add remaining sugar, beating until stiff peaks form. Fold egg whites into the rice, spoon into a buttered soufflé dish and bake in a cool oven for 1 hour.

VARIATIONS

The lime flavour can be omitted and lemon, vanilla, cinnamon or rum used instead.

Pineapple chicken with saffron rice

Baked ham and banana rolls

CURRIED SHARK

Preparation time 10 – 12 minutes
Cooking time about 30 minutes
To serve 4

You will need

2 lb. shark or other solid fish
1 tablespoon vinegar
1½ pints (U.S. 3¾ cups) water
3 cloves garlic, crushed
2 teaspoons powdered ginger or 2 slices fresh
    green ginger, finely chopped
1 teaspoon saffron strands
1½ teaspoons dry mustard
2 teaspoons curry powder
1 oz. ghee (see page 31) or butter or 2 table-
    spoons oil
2 onions, thinly sliced
3 green chillis, de-seeded and thinly sliced
    lengthways
1 tablespoon brown sugar

Clean, skin and bone the fish and cut into convenient-sized pieces. Bring to the boil with the vinegar and water and cook until tender, about 20 minutes according to the type of fish used.

Meanwhile, pound the garlic, ginger, saffron, mustard and curry powder and, using a few spoonsful of the fish stock, make it into a smooth paste. Drain the fish, retaining a little of the stock; put it on to a dish and coat each side liberally with curry mixture. Set aside for 10 minutes. While the fish marinates, heat the ghee, butter or oil and fry the onion rings in a large pan. Add the chillis and the coated fish and simmer over a low heat on each side for 5 minutes. This is a dry curry, but if the fish tends to stick, add a little of the fish stock. Sprinkle with brown sugar just before serving. Serve with plain boiled rice and mango chutney (see page 111).

Note
This is a light curry, not hot by West Indian standards, but it does add some excitement to a dull fish, such as cod; even frozen fish steaks take on a new aspect when cooked in this way.

HOT MEAT CURRY

Although saffron is expensive in Europe, it is quite cheap and plentiful in Grenada, where it grows. It is made from dried autumn crocus, which must be picked by hand. Each blossom has only three stigmas and statistics say that it needs seventy-five thousand blossoms to obtain one pound of saffron. Turmeric is more often used and is very similar in flavour and colour although the plant looks utterly different, a brilliant orange, very much like ginger in appearance.

Preparation time 10 minutes
Cooking time 1 – 1½ hours
To serve 4

You will need

1½ tablespoons vegetable oil
4 eschalots or spring onions, chopped
2 green chillis, de-seeded and chopped
2 tomatoes, peeled and chopped
1½ teaspoons coriander paste
½ teaspoon saffron strands
1 teaspoon powdered ginger
2 cloves garlic, finely chopped
1 stick celery, thinly sliced
2 tablespoons pepper
1 lb. beef, mutton or pork, cut into ½-inch cubes
1 pint (U.S. 2½ cups) water
½ pint (U.S. 1¼ cups) coconut water
1 lb. boiled rice, cooked with 6 cloves

Heat the oil in a large saucepan. Mix the eschalots or spring onions, chillis, tomatoes, coriander paste, saffron, ginger, garlic, celery and pepper. Put all these ingredients into the oil with the meat. Add water, bring to the boil and cook for 1-1½ hours, stirring from time to time to prevent burning. At the end of this time the meat should be cooked and all the water absorbed. Add the coconut water, stir again and cook for a further 3 minutes.

Heat the rice if it has become cold, arrange round the edge of a hot dish and pour the curry into the centre. Serve with chutney or plain yoghurt.

Note
For a milder curry, reduce the amount of pepper.

CURRIED ACKEE

Preparation time 7 minutes
Cooking time 25 – 30 minutes
To serve 4 – 5

You will need

6 ripe ackees
salt
1 oz. butter
1 tablespoon curry powder
1 onion, sliced
1 chilli, de-seeded and chopped
1 oz. flour
$\frac{1}{2}$ pint (U.S. $1\frac{1}{4}$ cups) coconut milk
squeeze lime juice

Remove pods, seeds and centres from ackees. Boil in salted water for 5 minutes, drain. Heat the butter, add the curry powder, sliced onions and chilli and cook for 5 minutes or until onion rings are transparent, but not brown. Stir in the flour, seasoned with salt and very slowly add the coconut milk, stirring all the time. Put the ackees in the sauce, add lime juice and simmer over a low heat for 15-20 minutes, until ackees are tender but still whole and the sauce is almost absorbed. Serve with plain boiled rice.
Note
Canned ackees can be bought at shops where West Indian foods are sold, giving everyone in most parts of the world a chance to taste this Jamaican tree vegetable.

CURRIED OMELETTE

Preparation time 7 – 10 minutes
Cooking time 15 minutes
To serve 4

You will need

FOR THE FILLING
1 oz. butter
2 onions, thinly sliced
$\frac{1}{2}$ teaspoon powdered turmeric
2 cloves garlic, chopped
2 green chillis, de-seeded and finely chopped
$\frac{1}{2}$ teaspoon powdered ginger
8 oz. cooked meat, chicken or ham, finely chopped
salt and pepper

FOR THE OMELETTE
4 or 5 eggs, according to size
1 tablespoon water
2 oz. butter

FOR THE FILLING
Melt butter in a frying pan and fry the onion rings until golden brown. Add the turmeric, garlic, chillis and ginger and cook over a high heat for 5 minutes, stirring all the time. If the mixture dries, add a little water. Add the meat and cook for a further 3 minutes until heated through. Season to taste with salt and pepper.

FOR THE OMELETTE
Beat the eggs lightly with the water. Heat the butter in an omelette pan until very hot, pour in the beaten egg and when it begins to set, put the curried meat almost in the centre. Fold the omelette over and serve. Cut into four slices, or, if preferred, make two omelettes quickly, dividing the meat between them and cutting each in half to serve.

VARIATION
This is also good with left-over fish, fresh or canned.

Curried omelette

FRUIT CURRY

Preparation time 10 minutes
Cooking time 1½ hours
To serve 4

You will need

2 onions, thinly sliced
1 oz. butter
1 small green chilli, de-seeded and finely
    chopped
2 tablespoons curry powder
1 teaspoon milk
2 slices pineapple, peeled and cut into pieces
1 small pawpaw, peeled, de-seeded and cut
    into pieces
2 bananas, peeled and roughly sliced
1 apple, cored and chopped (optional)
1 lime
1 pint (U.S. 2½ cups) coconut water
1 tablespoon coconut cream (see page 30)
1 oz. peeled ripe coconut, grated
½ teaspoon powdered ginger
20 stoned raisins
salt and pepper

Fry the onions in butter in a thick saucepan, add
the chilli pieces and brown them. Stir in the curry
powder and milk and cook, stirring, over a high
heat for 5 minutes. Mix the pineapple, pawpaw,
banana pieces and apple, if using, and squeeze the
lime over them before putting the fruit and coconut
water in the pan with the onion curry. Cook for a
further 10 minutes. Stir in the coconut cream, grated
coconut, ginger, raisins, salt and pepper. Stir
once, then simmer over a low heat for 1 hour.
Serve with plain boiled rice.
Note
This is a very good dish for vegetarians and can be
made with most of the fruit found in temperate
climates. Melon is a good substitute for the pawpaw
which can be bought tinned, and sometimes fresh,
away from the tropics. If liked, the raisins can be
soaked in rum to plump them; drain before adding
to the curry. For a dry curry, omit the coconut
water.

VEGETABLE CURRY

This is a basic curry method and almost any firm
vegetable can be used, marrow, cucumber, breadfruit, yam, English or sweet potatoes.

Preparation time 10 minutes
Cooking time 15 – 30 minutes
To serve 4 – 5

You will need

4 oz. peeled ripe coconut, grated
½ pint (U.S. 1¼ cups) coconut water
5 cloves garlic, finely chopped
1 teaspoon powdered ginger or 2 slices fresh
    green ginger, chopped
1 tablespoon crushed turmeric
2 red chillis, de-seeded and cut into small
    pieces
1½ lb. pumpkin, cut into 1-inch cubes
2 green chillis, de-seeded and cut into slices,
    lengthways
pinch salt
1 oz. ghee (see page 31) or butter or 2 table-
    spoons oil
1 onion, thinly sliced

Put the coconut to soak in the coconut water.
Pound garlic, ginger and turmeric with a pestle and
mortar. Put in a large saucepan with red chilli
pieces, coconut water, pumpkin and the green chilli
slices. Bring to the boil, season with a very little salt,
stir once, cover and simmer until the pumpkin is
just, but only just, tender; overcooking produces
soup.
While curry is cooking, heat ghee, butter or oil and
fry the onion rings until golden brown. Add the fat
and onion to the curry and cook for a further 3–5
minutes.

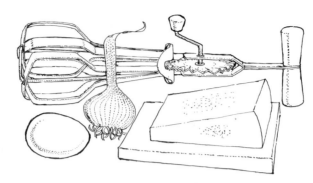

EGG AND CHEESE DISHES

Although chicken is usually abundant, eggs are unimportant on West Indian menus. Most cookbooks give only directions for fried, scrambled, poached or devilled eggs, although all mention egg nog (see page 124) which is the Christmas drink on some islands. However, the Chinese, of whom there are large contingents in Jamaica and Trinidad, use eggs in exciting ways and some of these recipes are included in this chapter.

Unless made at home by straining milk curd, all cheese is imported. The choice is somewhat limited by price, only the Cheddar type is cheap enough for everyday use.

The supermarkets usually display costly, and beautifully wrapped, fancy imported cheese which would not be suitable for cooking. I have, therefore, kept to recipes requiring only Cheddar type or Edam cheese, which is not so expensive on the Dutch islands. Dairy products are not, as yet, a strong point in the Caribbean, although strenuous efforts are being made to encourage farmers in that direction.

GROWN UP EGGS

This is a Chinese dish, sometimes called Iron Pot Eggs as the Chinese cook them in a metal pot.

Preparation time 10 – 12 minutes
Cooking time 30 minutes
To serve 4 – 6

You will need

10 eggs, well beaten
1 teaspoon salt
½ oz. lard, melted
8 oz. cooked minced pork
½ pint (U.S. 1¼ cups) water
2 tablespoons soy sauce

Blend all the ingredients thoroughly, then spoon into a fireproof dish with a lid. Cook over a low heat for 30 minutes.

By the time the eggs are cooked they will be blown up so that they push the cover off the dish and must be served immediately they are taken off the heat or they subside.

ONION EGGS ELEUTHERA

Eleuthera was one of the first Bahama islands to be colonised when the Eleutherian Adventurers, a Company formed in London in 1694, were shipwrecked off the northern tip. They named this island after the Greek word meaning *freedom*, most of their number being fugitives from Royalist religious persecution. Eleuthera to-day, is the main farming and agricultural island of the Bahamas, with plentiful dairy produce and superb pink sand beaches.

Preparation time 10 minutes
Cooking time 15 – 20 minutes
To serve 4

You will need

1 oz. butter
2 onions, thinly sliced
salt and pepper
pinch grated nutmeg
1 oz. flour
½ pint (U.S. 1¼ cups) milk
4 hard-boiled eggs, chopped
few drops Tabasco sauce

Melt the butter in a frying pan, add the onions and fry until golden brown. Season with salt, pepper and nutmeg. Stir in the flour, blending well over a low heat. Add the milk very slowly, stirring after each addition. Continue to cook over a low heat, stirring all the time, for 10 minutes. Remove from the heat stir in the eggs and serve in individual dishes with a drop or two of Tabasco on each. Serve hot or cold with plantain crisps (see page 17), or fingers of fried bread.

TABASCO OMELETTE LOAF

Preparation time 10 minutes
Cooking time 10 minutes
To serve 4 – 5

You will need

4 oz. soft breadcrumbs
1 green pepper, de-seeded and chopped
1 tomato, peeled and sliced
2 teaspoons chopped chives
4 drops Tabasco sauce
salt and pepper
8 eggs, separated
2 oz. butter

In a bowl, mix the breadcrumbs, pepper, tomato, chives and Tabasco. Season with salt and a little pepper. Beat the egg yolks and blend into the mixture. Whisk the whites until stiff and fold in. Heat the butter in a frying pan until very hot, toss in the egg mixture and with a wooden spoon or spatula, shape into a loaf. Cook for 10 minutes, turn on to a dish and serve cut in thick slices.

DOT HEART EGGS

Any number of servings can be boiled at the same time as this Chinese way of boiling eggs enables them to be kept, if necessary without refrigeration, for a day or two. In the tropics, I have found it better to keep them in the 'fridge and to immerse them in fresh water as they become rather too salty with keeping. They are eaten for breakfast, taken on picnics or used for snacks, known as a 'dot heart', or hunger appeaser. The eggs are almost soft centred again after this prolonged boiling.

Preparation time 1 minute
Cooking time 3 hours
To serve 12

You will need

12 eggs
1½ teaspoons salt
2 teaspoons tea
rind 1 tangerine

In a thick saucepan, boil the eggs in water for 1 hour. Drain them, immerse in cold water to cool, then tap gently to crack the shells, but do not peel them. Return to the saucepan with fresh water just to cover, bring to the boil and add the salt, tea and tangerine peel. Simmer over a very low heat for a further 2 hours. Remove from the heat but leave the eggs in the water in which they boiled the second time. Serve hot or cold.

Dot heart eggs

Sorrel eggs

SORREL EGGS

Sorrel does not grow on every Caribbean island, but I have made this pleasant dish in Jamaica and Grenada.

Preparation time 7 minutes
Cooking time 15 – 20 minutes
To serve 4

You will need

1 oz. butter
2 onions, finely grated
1 lb. sorrel leaves, callaloo or spinach, chopped
4 oz. peeled shrimps
$\frac{1}{4}$ pint (U.S. $\frac{2}{3}$ cup) cheese sauce (see page 28)
salt and pepper
4 eggs

Melt the butter in a saucepan, add the onions and cook for 3 minutes, stirring to prevent them from sticking to the bottom of the pan. Add the sorrel, callaloo or spinach, cover the pan and cook for 10 minutes uncovering from time to time to stir it. When the sorrel, callaloo or spinach is tender (this may take a little longer than 10 minutes if coarse) divide into four portions and put into four individual ovenproof dishes. Blend shrimps with the cheese sauce, season to taste with salt and pepper, and pour an equal quantity into each dish. Make a hollow, drop an egg into each, and put under the grill until eggs are set, about 2–3 minutes.

BANANA CHEESE SNACKS

Bananas are very much of a stand-by in the islands, nearly always available at a low price and tasting delicious, utterly different from those bought after the long frozen voyage across the Atlantic. To travel with the bananas, however, is a lively experience; whenever I see 'Fyffes' on a cardboard box on a wet day in England I think of the scene at Port Antonio, loading bananas in the United Fruit Company's dock.

Preparation time 5 – 8 minutes
Cooking time 10 minutes
To serve 4

You will need

3 oz. butter
4 oz. cheese, grated
4 large bananas, peeled and mashed
1 egg yolk
salt and pepper
made mustard
4 slices freshly made toast
1 teaspoon finely chopped parsley
1 teaspoon finely chopped chives

Melt 1 oz. butter in a saucepan, add the cheese and bananas and stir over a low heat for 5 minutes until well blended and creamy. Remove from the heat, stir in the egg yolk and season to taste with salt, pepper and mustard. Heat gently for a further 3–4 minutes, stirring all the time. Butter the toast, spread each slice with banana cheese mixture, sprinkle with chopped parsley and chives and brown under a hot grill for 1 minute.

CHEESE ICE CREAM

Preparation time 5 minutes
Cooking time 5 minutes
Oven temperature 425°F., Gas Mark 7
To serve 4 – 6

You will need

1 pint (U.S. $2\frac{1}{2}$ cups) single cream
$1\frac{1}{2}$ oz. strong cheese, grated, preferably Parmesan
pinch salt
pinch cayenne pepper
paprika

FOR THE WAFERS

12 unsweetend ice wafers
1½ oz. butter, melted
1½ oz. strong cheese, grated, as above

Set refrigerator to coldest setting. Blend the cream, cheese, salt and cayenne, beat well and pour into the freezing tray. Half-freeze the ice cream, remove from refrigerator, stir, sprinkle with paprika and freeze until firm.

FOR THE WAFERS

Brush the wafers with melted butter, sprinkle liberally with grated cheese, put on a baking sheet in a hot oven and bake for 5 minutes. Serve the ice sliced with the hot wafers.

Note

If unsweetened wafers are unobtainable, use any thin, unsweetened crackers to serve with the ice. Tinned grated Parmesan can be bought in most larger island supermarkets.

BARBADOS BREAD AND CHEESE SOUFFLE

This type of 'mock' soufflé is a good stand-by for unexpected guests or on early closing days and 'Banks' as the many holidays are called. Strangers to the islands may well be taken by surprise on Discovery Day, Independence Day, the Queen's Birthday, Thanksgiving Day or New Year's Day'.

Preparation time 10 minutes
Cooking time   20 – 25 minutes
Oven temperature 375°F., Gas Mark 5
To serve   4

You will need

8–10 slices white bread
1½ oz. butter
2 teaspoons made mustard
1 tablespoon finely chopped chives
4 oz. cheese, grated
1 egg
¼ pint (U.S. ⅔ cup) milk
salt and pepper

Grease an ovenproof dish with butter. Cut the crusts off the bread, butter each slice and spread with a little mustard. Cut into triangles, sprinkle with chives and arrange a layer of bread to cover the bottom of the dish. Sprinkle liberally with cheese and cover with a second layer of bread. Continue the layers of bread and grated cheese until the dish is nearly full. Beat the egg with the milk, season with salt and pepper and pour over bread. Bake in a moderately hot oven for 20–25 minutes, until the soufflé rises and is slightly browned on top. Serve very hot.

BAKED HAM AND BANANA ROLLS

(Illustrated in colour on page 38)

Preparation time 5 minutes
Cooking time   15 minutes
Oven temperature 375°F., Gas Mark 5
To serve   6

You will need

6 thin slices ham
1 teaspoon made mustard
6 firm bananas, peeled
¾ pint (U.S. 2 cups) cheese sauce (see page 28)

Spread ham slices with mustard and wrap each banana in ham. Put the ham and banana rolls into a shallow ovenproof dish, pour the sauce over and bake in a moderately hot oven for 10 minutes.

Fried flying fish

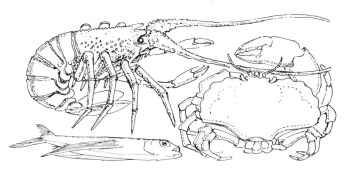

FISH

After rice, fish is the main source of protein and the most important island food. Price varies with the weather and size of the catch but it is usually cheap enough for everyone to afford. Bought on the beach or caught on one's line, nothing can touch Caribbean fish. Anything from a fishmonger's slab or frozen pack seems tame by comparison, but the culinary methods used by islanders make the very best use of fish, no matter where it comes from.

There are roughly four types of local fish; the dark, oily fish (dark because the oil is stored between the fibres), tuna, bonito and mackerel, for instance; the white fish, which store their oil in the liver, cod, dolphin, grouper, shark, snapper and flying fish. One sees flying fish in many parts of the Caribbean but they have become almost a national emblem in Barbados where the cry 'fish' means only *flying fish* and every child over ten can expertly scale and bone them. Shellfish are divided into crustaceans, such as crayfish, (which is what one usually has in the islands rather than lobster), shrimps, prawns and crab and molluscs, which live inside their shells, such as oysters (usually *tree* oysters, found on the mangrove bark in swamps), clams, turtle and sea eggs. The latter are fish which live inside a very pretty, round, spiky shell; one eats the roe but beware of the spikes, which are very painful if they get under the skin.

The usual cooking methods are by *baking*, the fish stuffed and sometimes foil-wrapped, or filleted and laid on a flat dish. Deep *frying* in oil or fat is best done in a wire basket; fried fish can be coated in egg and breadcrumbs or in batter, and shallow *frying* in black or clarified butter. *Grilling* is good for small whole fish or steaks, the fish brushed with melted butter and sprinkled with herbs and lime juice. Fish can also be *poached* or *steamed* but never boiled in water. Use a fish stock (see page 21) for poaching and put fish for steaming in a buttered steamer (or between two soup plates) over boiling water; sprinkle first with salt, pepper and lime juice.

Fish bought on the beach has to be cleaned; there are no fishmongers to clean fish in the islands. To clean, first cut off the fins, and trim the tail. Handle gently and use kitchen scissors rather than a knife. Hold the fish under water while the scales are scraped off with a blunt knife, then slit from just below the head to halfway down the underside; remove the guts but leave the roe. Cut off the head, or if the fish is the type where the head is left on, such as snapper and mackerel, cut off the gills. Wash again in running water and marinate, but never soak the fish. Finally, scour away any remaining dark skin with salt, season with a good squeeze of lime juice and cook within 15 minutes.

Boning is done after scaling. Cut off the head, then working from the centre of the back instead of the belly, slit with a sharp knife, pressing against the backbone. Lift out the bone, clean out the guts (using salt to scour) and divide into two or four fillets according to the size of the fish. Wash the fillets in running water and season with lime juice; the heads and bones are useful for stock. To stuff fish, slit one side, remove the guts and clean the cavity with salt and lime. Thread a darning needle with strong thread or double silk, stuff the fish and sew up; two stuffing mixtures will be found on page 54.

My local Speightstown market wakes up around 4 p.m. when the fishing boats put in; there is a great haggling between fishermen and the women who sell the fish. A tally man stands by as the great fish are put on the scales and when the argument grows too heated, it is usually he who decides the fisherman's price. Buying fish is not a quick business, I rarely go to the market and get just what I want in a matter of minutes.

FRIED FLYING FISH

Preparation time 5 minutes, plus 15 minutes
marinating
Cooking time 5 – 7 minutes
To serve 4

You will need

8 flying fish, scaled and boned (see page 47)
strained juice 2 limes
salt
1 onion, grated
2 teaspoons finely chopped thyme or marjoram
½ clove garlic, minced
2 eggs, lightly beaten
pepper
breadcrumbs or flour
fat or oil for frying

Marinate fish for 15 minutes in lime juice and salt.
Drain and dry. While fish is marinating, mix onion,
thyme or marjoram and garlic with a teaspoon of
salt and ¼ teaspoon pepper. Rub this into the fish,
especially the grooves left after boning. Dip in egg,
then dip in breadcrumbs, or flour if preferred, fry
on both sides in hot, shallow fat or oil. The fillets
should brown in 5 minutes. Serve with lime wedges.

MARINATED FLYING FISH

Preparation time 5 minutes, plus 5 hours marinating
To serve 4 – 6

You will need

6 – 8 flying fish, scaled and boned (see page 47)
strained juice 3 limes
salt
½ teaspoon olive oil
pepper

Cut the boned fish into four strips. Place on a soup
plate and sprinkle liberally with lime juice and
salt. Marinate for at least 5 hours in this mixture,
drain. Strain the lime juice, add the olive oil, drop
by drop, and the pepper. Arrange the fillets on a
dish and chill well before pouring over the dressing.

Pickled tuna

PICKLED TUNA

Preparation time 15 – 20 minutes
To serve 5 – 10

You will need

4 lb. middle-cut tuna fish with the bone
4 oz. salt
3 oz. castor sugar
1 tablespoon freshly ground pepper
1 teaspoon powdered allspice
3 small bunches tarragon or dill

Clean the fish and remove the bone very carefully
without breaking the fish. Rub the fillets with 1 oz.
salt to clean them and dry carefully. Blend 3 oz.
salt, the sugar, pepper and allspice and rub the
mixture all over the fish. Put one bunch of tarragon
or dill in the bottom of a dish or plate which is deep
enough to take the fillets one on top of the other. Put
the first fillet skin-side down on the tarragon or drill,
put a second bunch on top, cover with the second
fillet skin-side uppermost and put the third bunch
of tarragon or dill on top. Cover with a plate and
put a weight on top. Refrigerate for two days before
using; this fish will keep for a week in the 'fridge'.
Before serving, drain the fish liquid, scrape off the
tarragon or dill and lay the fillets side by side on a
wooden board. Slice diagonally, away from the
skin. Serves a first course for 10, or as a main course
for 5–6 with candied sweet potatoes (see page 81).
Note:
This way of pickling fish is good for any of the oily
fishes and is sometimes eaten like smoked salmon
with bread and butter and lime wedges.

Baked dolphin roe

BAKED DOLPHIN ROE

The local method of cooking roe is to fry it, but on the rather rare occasions when a friendly fisherman has parted with one, I have found this a very delicious way to cook it. The roe is known as 'The Caviar of Dolphin' and more often than not, the fisherman removes it before selling the fish. The roe of any large fish can be cooked in foil in the same manner.

Preparation time 10 minutes
Cooking time 20 – 25 minutes
Oven temperature 350°F., Gas Mark 4
To serve 4 – 6

You will need

1 or 2 dolphin roes, according to size
salt and pepper
strained juice 1 lime

FOR THE HERB BUTTER
2 oz. butter
1 tablespoon chopped thyme
1 tablespoon chopped parsley
1 tablespoon chopped marjoram

Rub the roe or roes all over with salt and pepper and sprinkle with lime juice.

FOR THE HERB BUTTER

Mix the butter with the chopped herbs. Cut a piece of foil the right size to envelop the roe completely. Spread the middle with half the herb butter mixture, put the roe or roes on top and dot with the remainder of the herb butter. Fold the foil and roll the edges tightly to seal, put on a baking sheet and bake in a moderate oven for 20–25 minutes according to the size of the roe. Serve with bread and butter and lime wedges as a main course or as an appetizer.

STEWED SHARK

Preparation time 10 minutes, plus 1 hour marinating
Cooking time 40 minutes
To serve 4 – 5

You will need

2 lb. shark, cleaned and cut into $1\frac{1}{2}$-inch thick slices
1 onion, sliced
1 teaspoon chopped chives
1 tablespoon chopped thyme
2 tablespoons vinegar
1 tablespoon rum
2 tablespoons olive oil
1 clove garlic, lightly crushed
1 oz. granulated sugar
1 tablespoon Worcestershire sauce
$\frac{1}{4}$ pint (U.S. $\frac{2}{3}$ cup) water
salt and pepper

Put the shark on a dish. Mix onion, chives, thyme, vinegar and rum, pour over the fish and marinate for 1 hour, turning after 30 minutes.
Heat the oil in a thick saucepan, add garlic and sugar and heat until it bubbles. Remove the garlic, take the fish from the marinade and drain, reserving the marinade. Fry fish in the oil for 5 minutes, browning a little on both sides. Add Worcestershire sauce and 3 tablespoons water to the marinade, pour this over the fish and simmer for 10 minutes. Sprinkle with salt and pepper to taste, add the rest of the water, cover the pan with a clean cloth (this makes more steam), put on the lid and cook gently for 20 minutes. Arrange the slices on a heated dish, pour the liquor from the pan over and serve with lime wedges.
Note
Shark is surprisingly delicate and light when well cooked.

MARRIED WOMEN
(Baked Jack)

Jacks vary in size from very small, not much bigger than sprats, to fish about the size of herring. In Grenada they are sometimes called 'Married Women', no one knows how they got this name.

Preparation time 10 – 12 minutes
Cooking time 20 – 25 minutes
Oven temperature 425°F., Gas Mark 7
To serve 4

You will need

salt and pepper
4 fairly large or 8 small jacks
½ pint (U.S. 1¼ cups) fish stock (see page 21)
strained juice 1 lime
1 oz. flour
2½ oz. butter
1 teaspoon finely chopped parsley
1 teaspoon finely chopped chives

Sift some salt and pepper together. Slash both sides of each fish three times and rub salt and pepper mixture into cuts. Grease a baking tin with butter, lay fish on it and pour over stock mixed with lime juice. Knead flour with 1 oz. butter and dot resulting paste on fish. Cover with buttered grease-proof paper and bake in a hot oven for 20 minutes, basting with melted butter. Put cooked fish on a dish and keep hot. Pour liquor from baking tin into a pan, add remaining butter, parsley and chives. Season with salt and pepper to taste and cook, stirring until sauce is reduced to two-thirds. Pour over fish and serve with slices of lime.

GRILLED TURTLE STEAK

Preparation time 5 – 7 minutes
Cooking time 20 – 25 minutes
To serve 4

You will need

1 oz. softened butter
4 turtle steaks, about 1½-inches thick, well cleaned
salt and pepper
strained juice 1 lime
2 teaspoons finely chopped parsley

Spread the softened butter on each side of the steaks. Grill under a hot grill for 10 minutes on each side. Season with salt and pepper, put on a heated dish and pour the pan juices over the turtle. Sprinkle a little lime juice and chopped parsley on each and serve with lime wedges.

TO PREPARE AND COOK SALT FISH

Soak salt fish overnight in cold water, drain. Put into a saucepan, covered with fresh cold water, bring to the boil and simmer for about 15 minutes until fish is tender. Skin and flake.
Note
Salt fish is best soaked overnight, but for quick de-salting, just cover with water in a saucepan, bring quickly to the boil and drain immediately.

CODFISH, CREOLE STYLE
(Illustrated in colour on page 56)

Preparation time 10 minutes
Cooking time 25 minutes
Oven temperature 375°F., Gas Mark 5
To serve 4

You will need

1 small onion, sliced
2 tomatoes, peeled and quartered
1 green pepper, de-seeded and chopped
large knob lard or bacon fat
8 oz. cooked salt fish, flaked (see above)
salt and pepper
8 oz. cooked yam or English potato, sliced
large knob butter
½ pint (U.S. 1¼ cups) milk
2 teaspoons parsley

Fry the onion, tomatoes and pepper in heated lard or bacon fat, add the fish and mix thoroughly. Season to taste. Arrange the yam or potato slices to cover the bottom and sides of a greased ovenproof dish. Pile in the fish mixture, dot with butter and pour over the milk. Sprinkle with parsley and bake in a moderately hot oven for 20 minutes.

Sunday breakfast

Salt fish pie

SUNDAY BREAKFAST

This is an after church, mid-morning breakfast dish that can be prepared in advance and takes only a short time to cook.

Preparation time 10 minutes
Cooking time 15 – 20 minutes
To serve 4

You will need

1½ lb. salt fish, soaked (see page 50)
4 English potatoes, peeled and sliced
2 onions, sliced
bacon fat for frying
2 hard-boiled eggs, halved lengthways
4 bananas, peeled and halved lengthways
pepper
1 tablespoon olive oil

Put fish into a saucepan with enough fresh water to cover. Add the potato slices, bring to the boil, cover and cook for 15 minutes or until potatoes and fish are tender. Meanwhile, fry the onion rings in bacon fat until golden brown and warm the eggs and bananas. Drain the fish and potatoes. Flake the fish, pile on to a heated dish with the potatoes and top with fried onion. Arrange the eggs and bananas around. Season lightly with pepper and pour the oil over just before serving.
Note
If fresh fish is used, do not, of course, soak it overnight, and add some salt to the water in which it is cooked.

SALT FISH PIE

Preparation time 10 – 15 minutes
Cooking time 30 minutes
Oven temperature 425°F., Gas Mark 7
To serve 4 – 5

You will need

1 oz. butter
1 hard-boiled egg, sliced
1 lb. cooked salt fish, flaked (see page 50)
2 small onions, sliced
3 tomatoes, sliced
1 small green pepper, de-seeded and chopped
1 raw egg, lightly beaten
¾ pint (U.S. 2 cups) milk
pinch salt and pepper
1 tablespoon Worcestershire sauce
8 oz. cooked English potatoes, mashed
1 oz. soft breadcrumbs
1 teaspoon chopped parsley

Grease a pie dish with the butter. Put in a few slices of hard-boiled egg, cover with layers of fish, the rest of the egg, onion rings, tomato slices and pepper pieces. Beat the raw egg in the milk, add the salt and pepper, beat lightly, then add the Worcestershire sauce and beat again. Pour the milk mixture over the fish. Spread mashed potato over the top, sprinkle with breadcrumbs and parsley and bake in a hot oven for 30 minutes.

TREE OYSTER AND OKRA STEW

The Caroni Swamp, near Port-of-Spain in Trinidad is known for its tree oysters. One can take a boat into the swamp and here, besides oysters and most beautiful tropical vegetation, the scarlet ibis make their nests. Any visitor to Trinidad should try to see this bird and to make the excursion to the swamp.

Preparation time 10 minutes
Cooking time   35 – 40 minutes
To serve   4 – 6

You will need

2 oz. butter
3 onions, chopped
3 tomatoes, peeled and chopped
½ pint (U.S. 1¼ cups) hot water
¼ pint (U.S. ⅔ cup) wine vinegar
dash cayenne pepper
1 teaspoon salt
1 teaspoon finely chopped sage
1 teaspoon finely chopped marjoram
8 oz. rice
pinch grated nutmeg
20 okras, thinly sliced
36 tree oysters, shelled and drained

Melt the butter in a saucepan and brown the onions lightly. Add the remaining ingredients, except the oysters and cook slowly over a low heat, stirring occasionally to prevent sticking, for 35 minutes. By this time the rice will be tender and the sauce thick. Remove from the heat, pour into a heated casserole or covered dish, add the oysters and allow to stand, covered, for 5 minutes before serving.

CONCH FRITTERS, ISLAND STYLE

Conch fritters are a great favourite with people in the Bahamas, where this shellfish is found in abundance. In Great Exuma, the Out-Island Regatta is held in April and during this period, the local conch seller makes fritters all day, starting at 6 a.m. and using about 50 conch. She showed me her method, smiling broadly 'Ever'body likes fritters, yez ma'am' she said.

Preparation time 8 minutes, plus 30 minutes resting
Cooking time   10 minutes
To serve   4 – 6

You will need

FOR THE BATTER
4 oz. flour
½ teaspoon salt
1 egg, lightly beaten
¼ pint (U.S. ⅔ cup) milk
1 onion, chopped
1 tomato, peeled and chopped
1 green pepper, de-seeded and chopped

FOR THE FILLING
1 lb. raw conch meat, cut into chunks
salt and pepper
deep fat or oil for frying

FOR THE BATTER
Sift the flour and salt together. Make a hollow in the middle and pour in the egg and half the milk. Beat well and gradually add the rest of the milk, onion, tomato and pepper pieces. Set the batter aside for 30 minutes.

FOR THE FILLING
Dry the conch chunks, season with salt and pepper and coat with batter. Fry in hot fat or oil and drain on absorbent paper.

Conch fritters, island style

Crab flan

CRAB FLAN

Preparation time 20 minutes, plus chilling time
Cooking time 35 minutes
Oven temperatures 425°F., Gas Mark 7
then
375°F., Gas Mark 5
To serve 4 – 6

You will need

8 oz. basic flan pastry (see page 91)

FOR THE FILLING
8 oz. cooked crab meat
2 teaspoons finely chopped parsley
1 teaspoon finely chopped chives
1 oz. butter
2 tablespoons white rum
2 egg yolks
generous $\frac{1}{4}$ pint (U.S. $\frac{3}{4}$ cup) white sauce
(see page 28)
salt and pepper
grated nutmeg

Roll out the pastry to a 10½-inch circle on a lightly floured board or marble slab. Lift into a 9-inch flan ring, placed on a baking sheet, or a flan tin, and trim edges. Roll out the trimmings, cut into thin strips and plait. Place round the edge of the flan and prick base. Chill. Fill the chilled flan case with greaseproof paper and rice and bake 'blind' in a hot oven for 10 minutes. Remove greaseproof paper and rice and bake for a further 5 minutes to dry out the base. Remove flan ring or tin.

FOR THE FILLING
Combine the crab meat, parsley and chives. Heat the butter in a saucepan and cook the crab mixture for 5 minutes. Sprinkle in the rum and pack into the pastry case. Beat the egg yolks with the sauce, season with salt and pepper and pour over the filling. Bake in a moderately hot oven for 25 minutes. Sprinkle with nutmeg before serving.

STUFFED CRAYFISH ANCHORAGE STYLE

This is a favourite dish at the Anchorage Hotel on Nassau's West Bay Street.

Preparation time 10 minutes
Cooking time 15 minutes
Oven temperature 375°F., Gas Mark 5
To serve 4

You will need

2 crayfish

FOR THE STUFFING
4 fillets flat fish, such as grouper, snapper or plaice
salt
pinch grated nutmeg
2 teaspoons finely chopped parsley
1 chilli, de-seeded and chopped
2 egg whites, very lightly beaten
3 tablespoons white rum
about 4 oz. soft breadcrumbs

Split the crayfish in half with a sharp knife, if possible while still alive, and extract the green meat, discarding the stomach and black thread. Leave the tails in the shells.

FOR THE STUFFING
Pound the fish fillets, mix with the green crayfish meat and season with a little salt and nutmeg. Blend in the parsley, chilli and egg whites, two tablespoons rum and enough breadcrumbs to make a pliable stuffing. Fill the gap between crayfish head and tail with this mixture.
Put on a baking sheet or ovenproof dish and bake in a moderately hot oven for 15 minutes. When the crayfish are cooked, put the remainder of the rum into a tablespoon, set it alight and pour over the fish, which should be served flaming.

CURRIED PRAWNS IN PINEAPPLE

(Illustrated in colour on page 55)

This is a recipe from the Trinidad Hilton, the famous 'upside down' hotel in Port-of-Spain. The main entrance is on the top floor while the bedrooms climb down the green hillside below.

Preparation time   15 – 20 minutes
Cooking time   30 – 35 minutes
To serve   4

You will need

FOR THE FILLING

1½ lb. live prawns or shrimps or 8 – 12 oz. peeled prawns or shrimps
salt (optional)
strained juice 1 lime (optional)
2 tablespoons olive oil
1 onion, chopped
1 tablespoon chopped chives, eschalots or spring onions
2 tomatoes, peeled and chopped
2 tablespoons curry powder
½ pint (U.S. 1¼ cups) fish stock (see page 21) or water
1 oz. butter
1 oz. flour
2 small pineapples

Scald the live prawns or shrimps in boiling salted water for 10 minutes. Drain, peel off the shell and head, slit the backs and remove the black cord. Clean in lime juice and salted water. Heat the oil in a frying-pan, add the onion, 1 teaspoon chives, eschalots or spring onions and tomato with the curry powder and cook for 5 minutes without browning. Add the stock or water and prawns and simmer over a low heat for 15 minutes. Remove from the heat. Blend butter and flour together and add in small pieces to prawns, stirring until smooth. Continue cooking for a further 3 minutes.
While the prawns are cooking, plunge the pineapples in boiling water for 3 minutes, drain. Halve them exactly down the middle leaving some leaves on each half, hollow out some of the flesh, fill the hollows with the prawn mixture and sprinkle with remaining chives, eschalots or spring onions. Allow half a pineapple per person.

STUFFINGS FOR BAKED FISH

FOR MEDIUM-SIZED FISH

Preparation time   5 minutes

You will need

4 oz. soft breadcrumbs
2 oz. butter, melted
1 tablespoon finely chopped chives
1 teaspoon finely chopped parsley
1 small green pepper, de-seeded and finely chopped
1 onion, grated
grated rind and strained juice 2 small limes
2 tablespoons minced ham
pinch grated nutmeg
salt and pepper

Blend all the ingredients together and mix well.

FOR LARGE FISH

Preparation time   5 – 7 minutes
Cooking time   7 minutes

You will need

4 rashers bacon
½ oz. butter
1 onion, grated
3 eggs, well beaten
8 oz. soft breadcrumbs
salt
black pepper or cayenne pepper
pinch grated nutmeg
1 large or 2 small cooked crabs, shelled

Remove rind from bacon and chop. Melt the butter in a saucepan, add the bacon and cook, stirring for 1 minute. Add the onion and cook for a further 3 minutes. Blend the eggs with the breadcrumbs, season with salt and black pepper or cayenne pepper and nutmeg. Stir into the bacon and onion mixture and cook for 1 minute. Pound crab meat, add to mixture and cook for a further 2 minutes, stirring well. Cool the stuffing before use.

Curried prawns in pineapple

Codfish, Creole style

Baked Christmas ham and Christmas egg nog

Caribbean kebabs

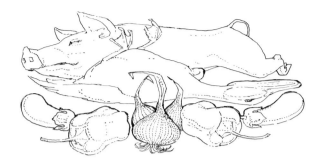

MEAT AND POULTRY

After rice and fish, meat comes third for the islanders, whose dishes tend to be spicy. Some recipes stem from tradition and folklore, the New Year sucking pig, for instance, is said to bring good luck if it is the first morsel eaten after midnight. Turkey is served not only at Christmas, but as the focal point of the wedding breakfast or family gathering. Baked ham, the traditional Christmas dish in Trinidad, crops up in this capacity on other islands; chicken appears everywhere on any day of the week. Goat or mutton is the meat of the Jamaican people; in small villages one may see a sign 'Curried goat to-day' very much like 'Fish frying' in some shop windows in England; I was offered 'Goat Water' in Montserrat which sounded unpalatable but proved to be a tasty stew. There are wild birds to be shot in the swamps and forests; duck, goose, pigeon and teal. Coconuts can be used for veal or chicken for an elusive flavour.

There is still a wild boar hunt in Portland parish, Jamaica, near Port Antonio in the Swift River area. In the past, many a buccaneer lived on wild boar, smoking it slowly over a fire which was known as the *boucan*, and from which their name derived.

Arawaks and Caribs, the original people of the islands, ate agouti, a rare specimen still sometimes found in the Bahama out-islands; Columbus referred to them as 'barkless dogs', a cross between rat and rabbit whose delicate flavour appealed to his men. Not every island can produce a butcher. Sophisticated islands have those who can prepare rib roast and sirloin and the rest of the cuts, but many simply chop up meat; in the latter case stews are the safest dishes to prepare with it.

To be certain of tender meat, take it from the freezer in which it will have been stored, allow it to defrost slowly and then wrap in pawpaw skins, rubbing in the seeds. Two hours is the maximum for pawpaw treatment and it should be discarded before marinating.

For good quality meat, searing in a very hot oven 475°F., Gas Mark 9 for 25 minutes until it is brown, gives a good flavour; then reduce heat to 300°F., Gas Mark 2, allowing 20 minutes per pound for rare meat and 30 for well done, the searing time included. Meat for grilling should be brushed with butter or oil, seasoned and cooked quickly to retain juices in a crisply brown outside; poultry is grilled more slowly but still prepared in the same manner.

The meat in the islands is frequently grilled over charcoal which imparts a delicious flavour, but if cooked in this way, it must be basted frequently during cooking.

Roast chicken tends to dry and should be cooked slowly with a dab of butter inside as well as stuffing and should be basted frequently. Turkey should be covered with greaseproof paper to prevent too much browning, goose requires no basting or added fat, but duck needs basting. For teal or pigeon, tie a bacon rasher over the breast.

Boiled fowl should be slowly simmered in water or stock, brought to boiling point before immersing. The timing is 25 minutes to the pound.

As with other foods, there is no one particular method of cooking the Caribbean way; I have chosen the more original and useful meat dishes found in the galaxy of islands.

CARIBBEAN KEBABS

(Illustrated in colour on page 58)

Preparation time 10 minutes, plus 8 hours
marinating
Cooking time 10 – 15 minutes
To serve 4

You will need

FOR THE MARINADE

1 oz. butter
2 onions, chopped
½ clove garlic, chopped
2 mangoes
½ teaspoon salt
pinch cayenne pepper
2 tablespoons curry powder
2 tablespoons vinegar
2 oz. brown sugar

FOR THE SKEWERS

1½ lb. any grilling meat, cut into 1½-inch cubes
2 firm ripe bananas
12 cubes peeled ripe pineapple
12 cubes peeled firm ripe pawpaw

FOR THE MARINADE

Heat the butter, fry the onion and garlic until
brown, Peel mangoes, remove stones and mash.
Add mango pulp, salt, cayenne, curry powder,
vinegar and sugar to onion, mix well and put on to a
soup plate.

FOR THE KEBABS

Put the meat cubes into the marinade and leave
overnight in the refrigerator.
Drain the meat when required the next day and
reserve the marinade. Thread the cubes on to
skewers with alternate pieces of banana, pineapple
and pawpaw. Brown the meat, turning on each of
the four sides, under a hot grill. Add the pan
drippings to the marinade, heat and pour over the
skewers. Serve with plain boiled rice.
Note
This dish can be made with apricots in place of
mango and pawpaw can be omitted if unobtainable.

MEAT LOAF

Ask any Barbadian cook "What shall we have today?" and the chances are she will reply "Meat loaf,
please" or "Meat balls". The balls can be made from
the same ingredients, shaped into balls, rolled in
flour and fried in deep fat.

Preparation time 10 minutes
Cooking time 1 hour 20 minutes
Oven temperature 375°F., Gas Mark 5
To serve 4 – 6

You will need

1 lb. minced raw beef
1 lb. minced raw pork
4 oz. soft breadcrumbs
4 – 5 tablespoons milk
salt and pepper
½ teaspoon finely chopped thyme
½ teaspoon finely chopped chives
½ teaspoon finely chopped parsley
4 tablespoons brown sauce (see page 27)
2 eggs, lightly beaten
1 oz. flour
2 oz. butter
dash Tabasco sauce

TO GARNISH
parsley sprigs

Mix the beef and the pork thoroughly. Moisten the
breadcrumbs with milk and add to the minced
meat. Season with salt, pepper, thyme, chives and
parsley. Stir in the sauce and bind with the eggs,
beating them into the mixture. Shape into a loaf
and dust the top with half the flour. Melt the butter
in a baking tin, put in the loaf and bake in a moderately hot oven for 1¼ hours. When cooked, remove
and drain the loaf; keep hot on a dish. Stir the
remaining flour into the pan juices, add Tabasco
and cook until thick and light brown. Serve very
hot with the meat loaf. Serve meat loaf sliced and
garnished with parsley.
Note
This dish is very good cold with salad or the left-over
slices can be used for sandwiches.

Caribbean pepperpot

CARIBBEAN PEPPERPOT

This pepperpot recipe is the one most used in the Eastern Caribbean but recipes vary greatly from island to island. In Jamaica, it is a soup, in Guyana the basis is chicken or oxtail with sugar, cassareep and chillis added.

Preparation time   10 minutes
Cooking time   2½ – 3 hours
To serve   4 – 5

You will need

8 oz. salt pork
8 oz. salt beef
1 lb. fresh meat
1½ pints (U.S. 3¾ cups) cold water
1 teaspoon salt
6 callaloo leaves, chopped with their stems
4 aubergines, sliced
2 onions, sliced
1 lb. pumpkin, diced
2 tomatoes, sliced
1 tablespoon chopped chives
1 tablespoon chopped thyme
6 okras, sliced
pepper
1 lb. cooked pigeon peas

Wash the meat and chop roughly into convenient pieces, about 1½-inches square. Put in a large, heavy saucepan, cover with some of the water and bring very slowly to the boil. When just beginning to boil, add salt and continue simmering over a low heat for at least 1½ hours. Skim the scum from the surface, add a little more cold water, skim again and repeat this process three times. Add all the vegetables and seasonings, except the peas and simmer for a further 1 hour, skimming from time to time if more scum rises. Stir in the peas, cook for a further 5 minutes and serve very hot with plenty of pepper added.
Note
Spinach can be used in place of callaloo and split peas instead of pigeon.

AUBERGINE BEEF PIE

Preparation time   20 minutes
Cooking time   40 minutes
Oven temperature   375°F., Gas Mark 5
To serve   4

You will need

1 large aubergine
1 oz. bacon fat or lard
1½ lb. minced raw beef
2 onions, grated
½ clove garlic, crushed
1 tablespoon finely chopped parsley
1 teaspoon finely chopped marjoram
salt and pepper
pinch grated nutmeg
2 tablespoons tomato ketchup
1 cooked breadfruit, yam or large English potato, mashed
1½ oz. crisp breadcrumbs (raspings)
½ oz. butter

Peel aubergine, slice and cut slices into strips about 1-inch wide. Fry them in fat for about 5 minutes, or until tender, shaking constantly to prevent them from sticking to the pan. Mix beef, onions, garlic, parsley and marjoram and season with salt, pepper and nutmeg. Grease a pie dish and cover the bottom with a layer of the beef mixture, cover with fried aubergine moistened with tomato ketchup. Continue the layers until the dish is nearly full, then top with finely mashed breadfruit. Sprinkle with breadcrumbs, dot with butter and bake in a moderately hot oven for 40 minutes.

PUERTO RICAN POT ROAST

Preparation time 25 minutes
Cooking time $2\frac{3}{4} - 3\frac{1}{4}$ hours
To serve 8

You will need

4 lb. topside
2 oz. salt pork, skinned and chopped
1 teaspoon chopped capers
1 teaspoon chopped oregano
1 teaspoon vinegar
2 green peppers, de-seeded and chopped
3 chillis
2 onions, chopped
3 tablespoons olive oil
2 oz. lard
$2\frac{1}{2}$ pints (U.S. $6\frac{1}{4}$ cups) water
1 tablespoon salt
$1\frac{1}{2}$ lb. English potatoes, peeled and diced
1 tomato, chopped
3 tablespoons tomato purée

Make a deep cut with a sharp knife across the meat. Combine pork, capers, oregano and vinegar with half the peppers, chillis and onions and 1 tablespoon oil. Pound to a smooth mixture and stuff this into the joint. Melt the lard in a large saucepan and brown the meat on all sides over a high heat for

Puerto Rican pot roast

10 minutes. Add the water, salt and remaining peppers, chillis and onions, bring to the boil and simmer over a moderate heat for $2-2\frac{1}{4}$ hours. Add the potatoes, tomato and tomato purée, mixed with the rest of the olive oil. Stir into the pot, bring back to the boil and cook uncovered for a further 30 minutes or until potatoes are soft and the sauce thickens.
Note
This kind of pot roast is very satisfactory cooked in a pressure cooker, reducing the cooking time by a third.

GOAT WATER

This is the popular stew of Montserrat, where it might be washed down with 'Plastic', not a brightly coloured drink, but a fiery, raw local rum.

Preparation time 7 – 10 minutes
Cooking time 2 hours
To serve 4 – 5

You will need

1 oz. butter
2 onions, sliced
2 lb. goat, cut into cubes
3 cloves
1 clove garlic, chopped
2 tomatoes, thickly sliced
salt and pepper
cayenne pepper
1 pint (U.S. $2\frac{1}{2}$ cups) water
1 tablespoon flour
2 tablespoons tomato ketchup
dash Tabasco sauce

Melt the butter in a thick saucepan, cook the onions in it until clear but not brown, then add the meat and brown quickly. Add cloves, garlic, tomato slices, salt, pepper and a pinch of cayenne. Cover with water, bring to the boil, then reduce heat and simmer very slowly for 2 hours, skimming from time to time. Fifteen minutes before end of cooking time, pour off enough stock to make a paste with the flour, add the tomato ketchup and a dash of Tabasco, stir the paste into the stew and continue stirring until well blended and the stew thickens. Adjust seasoning and serve with rice, sweet potatoes or yams.

Creole roast lamb

Pigs' tails

CREOLE ROAST LAMB

Preparation time 5 minutes
Cooking time   about 1 hour 10 minutes
Oven temperature 400°F., Gas Mark 6
To serve   6 – 8

You will need

1 tablespoon vinegar
2 tablespoons Worcestershire sauce
1 teaspoon cassareep (optional)
dash Tabasco sauce
2 teaspoons chopped thyme
½ bay leaf, pounded
salt and pepper
½ pint (U.S. 1¼ cups) boiling stock (see page 21)
2 onions, grated
1 clove garlic, crushed
1 small leg of lamb

Stir the vinegar, Worcestershire sauce, cassareep (this makes the sauce dark brown but other colourings may be used instead), Tabasco, thyme, bay leaf and a pinch of salt and pepper into the hot stock. Add the onions and garlic and cook for 5 minutes. Rub the lamb with salt and pepper and roast in a moderately hot oven (allowing 20 minutes to the pound and 25 minutes over), basting frequently with the stock mixture. When the lamb is cooked, slice what is required, arrange on a heated dish, drain the fat from the pan and mix with any unused basting mixture. Reheat, season a little more if required and pour over the sliced meat.

PIGS' TAILS

Strangers may reject pigs' tails which are in every island shop, even the most modern supermarkets. This recipe is not the same as the local one, but it makes an appetising and inexpensive meal.

Preparation time 5 – 7 minutes
Cooking time   35 – 55 minutes
To serve   4

You will need

4 pigs' tails
salt
1 oz. butter
½ pint (U.S. 1¼ cups) stock (see page 21)
2 egg yolks, lightly beaten
1 teaspoon chopped chives
½ green pepper, de-seeded and chopped
dash Tabasco sauce

Trim and wash the tails, put them in a saucepan covered with salted water and simmer for 35-55 minutes according to size, or until tender. Drain and dry but keep the tails hot. Melt the butter in a frying pan and cook until a light brown, add the stock and cook until reduced to nearly half. Add the egg yolks, scraping the bottom of the pan to prevent sticking and stirring all the time until the sauce is quite thick. Do not allow to boil after the egg yolks have been added. Add chives, pepper and Tabasco, and stir again. Serve the pigs' tails on a bed of Peas An' Rice (see page 143) and either pour the sauce over or serve separately.

FESTAL SUCKING PIG

In the islands the pig is often spit roasted over a charcoal grill.

Preparation time about 30 minutes
Cooking time about 4 hours
Oven temperature 375°F., Gas Mark 5
To serve 12 – 16

You will need

FOR THE STUFFING
1¼ lb. soft breadcrumbs
4 tablespoons rum
4 tablespoons lard or dripping
1 onion, minced
1 clove garlic, minced
1 tablespoon powdered ginger
1½ teaspoons salt
1 tablespoon pepper
2 teaspoons chopped thyme
pinch grated nutmeg
grated rind 1 lime
1 oz. stoned raisins, chopped
1 tablespoon Worcestershire sauce
1 egg, lightly beaten (optional)

FOR THE PIG
1 sucking pig, about 10 lb., prepared for roasting with offal separate
vinegar
salt and pepper
1 clove garlic, cut
rum
butter or oil
½ pint (U.S. 1¼ cups) water

FOR THE GRAVY
pig's heart and liver
1 pint (U.S. 2½ cups) water
1 onion, minced
1 teaspoon finely chopped parsley
1 small green pepper, de-seeded and chopped
1 oz. flour
salt and pepper

TO GARNISH
1 unripe otaheite apple, firm orange or tomato
4 roasted plantains or green bananas
4 stuffed green peppers
4 slices grilled pineapple, halved
heated oil for rubbing

FOR THE STUFFING
Moisten the crumbs with rum. Heat the lard or dripping and fry onion and garlic. Stir in the moistened crumbs and add ginger, salt, pepper, thyme, nutmeg and lime rind. Cook over a low heat for about 5 minutes or until all the fat is absorbed. Remove from the heat, stir in the raisins and Worcestershire sauce and beat in the egg if liked. (The egg helps to bind the mixture which should be soft and crumbly.)

FOR THE PIG
Wash the pig in several waters and wipe with a cloth wrung out in vinegar. Rub all over with salt, pepper and garlic, then brush with rum inside and out. Stuff loosely, and sew up the opening with a trussing needle and thread. Prop open the mouth with a piece of wood or other suitable utensil, tie the forelegs together and hind legs under the belly. Wipe once again with the vinegar cloth and brush with melted butter or oil (oil gives a crisper finish). Score the back in several places with a sharp knife and cover the ears with foil to prevent scorching. Roast in a moderately hot oven for about 3½ hours, or until nearly tender and fairly brown, basting frequently with the fat in the pan to which the water has been added. Cover with foil for the final 30 minutes, or sooner if the pig is too brown. Cooking time will depend on the pig, but for a baby pig, 20 minutes per pound, plus an extra 30 minutes should be right.

FOR THE GRAVY
While the pig is roasting, simmer the heart in the water until nearly tender, about 1¼-1¾ hours, depending on size, then add the liver and simmer until both are cooked. Add onion, parsley and pepper and simmer gently for 10 minutes. Drain the offal, reserving the stock. Chop offal finely and add to the pan in which the pig is roasting with ½ pint (U.S. 1¼ cups) of the stock in which they were cooked. Finish roasting the pig if it is not yet tender. Take the pig from pan, put it on to a heated dish and keep warm. Skim the fat from the pan liquid, stir in the flour, scraping the bottom of the pan, season with salt and pepper and simmer for about 4 minutes until light brown and slightly thickened. Season to taste and serve separately.

TO GARNISH
Take the prop out of the pig's mouth and insert an otaheite apple, orange or tomato (or any brightly coloured fruit). Arrange plantains, peppers and pineapple around the dish. Rub the pig very gently with oil to make it glisten, put a flower in each ear and a chain of flowers around the neck.

BAKED CHRISTMAS HAM

(Illustrated in colour on page 57)

Preparation time 10 minutes
Cooking time about 1¼ hours
Oven temperature 300°F., Gas Mark 2
To serve 8 – 10

You will need

4 – 5 lb. ham
pepper
cloves
4 oz. brown sugar and 1 teaspoon dry mustard
   or ½ pint (U.S. 1¼ cups) pineapple juice

TO GARNISH
10 slices pineapple
2 red peppers, de-seeded and sliced

Soak ham overnight in cold water to cover, drain and dry. Season the ham with pepper and put it, fat side uppermost, on a rack in a baking tin. Bake in a cool oven for about 1¼ hours (allow 20 minutes to the pound and 20 minutes over). Thirty minutes before end of cooking, take the ham from the oven pull off the skin and drain off the fat from the pan. Score the ham fat in a diamond pattern, sticking a clove into each diamond. Mix together sugar and mustard, blend to a paste with 2 tablespoons of the drained fat from the ham, pour this mixture over the ham and return to the oven to finish baking. Alternatively, pour pineapple juice over the ham, but this does not give it the glaze of the sugar and mustard.
Add pineapple and pepper slices to the pan for the last 10 minutes cooking. Serve the ham garnished with the pineapple and pepper slices.
Note
This is the Christmas dinner dish in Trinidad where every relative is visited sometime during the day.

Baked ham is delicious at any time of year, hot or cold; canned ham can be glazed in the same manner, just giving it the final 30 minutes in the oven.

CHICKEN IN COCONUTS

Preparation time 20 minutes
Cooking time 20 minutes
To serve 6

Chicken in coconuts

You will need

2 large ripe coconuts
1 small pawpaw or melon
1 oz. flour
1 teaspoon salt
½ teaspoon pepper
pinch paprika
pinch powdered ginger
2 teaspoons finely chopped thyme
1½ – 2 lb. cooked chicken, diced
2½ oz. butter
3 tablespoons rum
¼ pint (U.S. ⅔ cup) brown sauce (see page 27)
4 tablespoons single cream

With a skewer, pierce the three eyes at one end of the coconuts. Empty the milk into a jug. Eye end down, put the coconuts on a hard surface, tap with a hammer and they will split in half. Scrape out the flesh, remove brown skin, grate and toast until golden under a hot grill, shaking so that it browns evenly. Halve the pawpaw, or melon, scoop out the seeds and with a potato baller, scoop out the flesh in small balls (neat cubes can be used instead).
Mix the flour with salt, pepper, paprika, ginger and thyme and coat the chicken well in seasoned flour. Heat the butter in a saucepan and fry the chicken for 3 minutes. Stir in the rum, ¼ pint (U.S. ⅔ cup) coconut milk, brown sauce and cream. Simmer over a low heat, stirring constantly, for 10 minutes, until the sauce is thick and smooth. Fill each empty half coconut with chicken mixture, garnish with pawpaw or melon balls, sprinkle with some of the grated coconut and serve remainder separately. Serve with breadfruit crisps (see page 18).

DEVILLED CHICKEN PARTS

Preparation time 5 minutes
Cooking time   35 minutes
To serve   4

You will need

2½ oz. butter
1½ lb. chicken parts, preferably wings
4 oz. crisp breadcrumbs (raspings)
3 tablespoons vinegar
1 clove garlic
1 bay leaf
¼ teaspoon salt
1 teaspoon paprika
½ teaspoon pepper
pinch cayenne pepper
3 tablespoons tomato sauce (see page 27)
dash Tabasco sauce

Heat half the butter until foaming, cook the chicken pieces in this until golden. Remove from the pan and roll in breadcrumbs until thickly coated, then return to the butter and cook for about another 20 minutes until the breadcrumbs are crisp and the chicken tender. Add a little more butter if required. When cooked, take the chicken from the pan, drain and keep hot. Add the vinegar, garlic, bay leaf, salt, paprika, pepper and cayenne to the butter remaining in the pan. Simmer over a low heat until reduced to about half, then discard the garlic and

bay leaf. Add the tomato sauce, Tabasco and remaining butter. Stir until smooth and piping hot. Arrange the chicken pieces on a heated dish, pour over the sauce and serve with fried bananas.
Note
Chicken parts, as they are called, are sold everywhere, usually wrapped and frozen, with the wings and legs separate.

COLD CRYSTAL CHICKEN

I learnt this very effective and economical way of cooking chicken from Wong, a Chinese Jamaican cook. The chicken, however, must be tender and sometimes I give mine the pawpaw treatment (see page 59) for an hour before cooking.

Preparation time 5 – 8 minutes
Cooking time   8 – 10 minutes, plus
                   cooling time
To serve   4 – 6

You will need

2 pints (U.S. 5 cups) fast boiling water
1 slice green ginger (optional)
1 onion, sliced
1 small young chicken
2 oz. butter
salt and pepper
1 teaspoon finely chopped chives

Devilled chicken parts

Make sure the water is boiling fast, then add the ginger and onion. While the water comes back to fast boiling, insert three metal teaspoons inside the chicken (or 2 spoons if it is very small), put the whole bird into fast boiling water to cover and bring once again to the boil. Boil for 5 minutes, then cover the saucepan with a clean cloth and put the lid on. Turn off the heat and leave the chicken in the pan until absolutely cold. It will then be just nicely cooked, the spoons acting as heat conductors. Drain the chicken, melt the butter, add salt and pepper to taste and chives, and lightly brush over the chicken.

VARIATION

If preferred, the butter may be omitted and a sauce made by cooking the chives in 2 tablespoons peanut oil and stirring in 2 tablespoons soy sauce. Chill the sauce and serve with the cold chicken.

TURKEY ROLLS

Preparation time 10 minutes
Cooking time about 10 minutes
To serve 4 – 6

You will need

scant 1 oz. butter
2 onions, finely chopped
1½ tablespoons flour
1 teaspoon finely chopped parsley
1 teaspoon finely chopped chives
½ teaspoon powdered thyme
pinch ground mace
¼ pint milk
2 egg yolks
1 lb. finely minced cooked turkey
salt and pepper
dash Tabasco sauce
4 oz. soft breadcrumbs
4 oz. blanched peanuts, finely chopped
1 whole egg
1 tablespoon tomato ketchup
deep fat or oil for frying

Heat butter in a saucepan and cook onions until transparent, but not brown. Stir in flour, parsley, chives, thyme and mace. Add milk gradually, stirring all the time until the sauce is quite smooth. Remove from heat and add egg yolks, lightly beaten, stirring each in separately. Add the turkey, beat well and season with salt, pepper and Tabasco. Spread the turkey paste on to a plate to cool.

Form the mixture into sausage-shaped rissoles. Mix the breadcrumbs and peanuts thoroughly and roll the rissoles until they are coated with the mixture. Mix the whole egg with tomato ketchup, beat lightly and roll the coated rolls in the egg mixture. Roll again in breadcrumbs and peanut coating. Fry in hot deep fat or oil until golden brown, drain and serve hot on a bed of callaloo or spinach with Peanut Sauce (see page 28).
Note
If salted peanuts are used, adjust the final seasoning accordingly or wash off the salt before chopping.

DEVILLED TURKEY LEGS

On Boxing Day, in almost all the islands, there is some kind of local band which plays from house to house or in the streets. As far off as Bermuda, there are 'Gombies', boys in feathered headdress and costumes sewn with mirror fragments; in the Bahamas and Jamaica, there are the 'Junkanoos', or 'John Canoos', derived from the French 'inconnu' (unknown or masked). In Antigua and Montserrat, the Whip Dancers perform their pure African movements in teams on the beaches, in the Virgin Islands, the Fungi bands, ('fungi' meaning country style) play their shrill pipes. On almost every island 'scratch' bands and the dancers go their rounds, masked and padded and wearing some sort of headdress. Boxing Day is a day to go out, to go on the beach or for a picnic, so turkey legs are ideal for lunch.

Preparation time 5 minutes, plus overnight
marinating
Cooking time about 10 minutes
To serve 4

You will need

4 cooked turkey legs
salt and pepper
pinch cayenne pepper
1 tablespoon dry mustard
1 tablespoon Worcestershire sauce

Score the turkey legs, making deep regular cuts in four places. Season with salt and pepper and cayenne. Mix the mustard with Worcestershire sauce and coat the legs with the mixture. Leave in the refrigerator overnight and the next day, grill under a hot grill until crisp and brown. Serve with fried plantains or green bananas.

CONDADO DUCK

Condado used to be the smartest area of San Juan, the 'Platinum Coast' of Puerto Rico. Skyscrapers still rise from the Atlantic coast but some of the great hotels have fallen on hard times. This recipe came from the old Condado Beach Hotel where, at one time, cuisine and service equalled the best European standards, a rarity in the Caribbean.

Preparation time 15 – 20 minutes
Cooking time $1\frac{1}{2}$ – $1\frac{3}{4}$ hours
To serve   6 – 8

You will need

3 tablespoons olive oil
2 tablespoons paprika
4 – 5 lb. duck, jointed
1 onion, chopped
1 oz. flour
1 pint (U.S. $2\frac{1}{2}$ cups) chicken or beef stock
  (see page 21)
$\frac{1}{2}$ teaspoon salt (optional)
4 tablespoons rum
1 tomato, sliced
1 green pepper, de-seeded and very thinly
  sliced
2 teaspoons finely chopped parsley

Blend the oil and half the paprika, heat the mixture and fry the duck until brown all over. Remove the duck pieces, add the onion to the oil and cook for 5 minutes. Stir in the flour, then add the stock very slowly (a little salt may be used to season the stock if desired), stirring all the time. Add the rum and cook over a low heat, stirring, for about 2 minutes until the sauce is very smooth and thick. Add the duck, tomato and pepper, cover and cook over a low heat for 1-$1\frac{1}{4}$ hours or until duck is tender. Sprinkle with parsley and the rest of the paprika just before serving.

BLUE MOUNTAIN PIGEON

Preparation time 10 minutes, plus 30 minutes
                            marinating
Cooking time   27 – 30 minutes
To serve   4

You will need

2 pigeons
$\frac{1}{4}$ pint (U.S. $\frac{2}{3}$ cup) olive oil
2 tablespoons chopped parsley
1 tablespoon chopped chives
salt and pepper
black butter (see page 31)

Carefully split the pigeons from the back without separating the halves. Flatten them with a broad knife. Mix the oil, parsley and chives, season the birds with salt and pepper and marinate them in the oil for 30 minutes, turning them twice.
Skin side down, grill the birds under a moderate heat for 15 minutes, basting with the marinade; then turn them and grill for a further 10 minutes or until they are tender. Finish quickly under a high heat for about 2 minutes. Put a pat of black butter on each and serve with lime wedges and breadfruit crisps (see page 18).

Condado duck

68

SWEET POTATO STUFFING FOR CHICKEN OR TURKEY

Preparation time   5 minutes
Cooking time   12 – 15 minutes
To stuff   a 5 – 6 lb. chicken

You will need

8 oz. sausage meat
1 onion, chopped
8 oz. soft breadcrumbs
3 cooked sweet potatoes, mashed (see below)
pinch grated nutmeg
pinch chopped thyme
2 cloves
salt and pepper

Cook sausage meat for 10 minutes over a low heat. Add remaining ingredients and cook for a further 2-3 minutes. Cool and remove cloves before using.
Note
Use double above quantity for a turkey. Yam and sweet potato become hard when cold, therefore reheat or have freshly mashed sweet potatoes for stuffing.

MANGO RICE STUFFING FOR DUCK OR GOOSE

Preparation time   5 – 7 minutes
To stuff   a 4 lb. duck

You will need

2 large or 3 small mangoes
1 lb. cold cooked rice
1½ oz. butter, melted
2 teaspoons finely chopped parsley
1 teaspoon finely chopped chives
2 teaspoons finely chopped thyme
¼ teaspoon grated nutmeg
2 cloves
salt and pepper

Peel mangoes, remove stones and mash to a pulp. Blend all the ingredients thoroughly, seasoning with salt and pepper to taste. Chill before using and remove the cloves before stuffing the bird.
Note
Use double the above quantity to stuff a goose. Apricots, ripe peaches or prunes may be used in place of mangoes. This stuffing is also good with pork and veal.

PEPPERY QUAIL (OR TEAL)

In the Cayman Islands there is autumn shooting of quail, teal and baldpate.

Preparation time   7 minutes, plus 2 hours
                    soaking
Cooking time   about 20 minutes
To serve   4

You will need

4 onions
vinegar
4 quail
2 tablespoons pepper
2 tablespoons curry powder
2½ oz. butter

Boil the onions until soft, drain and soak in vinegar for 2 hours. Clean the quail and stuff each with an onion. Mix the pepper and curry powder thoroughly. Melt the butter and brush all over each bird. Dip them in the pepper and curry mixture and grill under a high heat until they are tender and brown. Baste with a little more butter if they tend to dry and sprinkle again with pepper mixture just before serving. Serve with plantain crisps (see page 17).

VEGETABLES AND SALADS

The great difference in Caribbean vegetables is what they are called and names vary from island to island. Root vegetables, known as 'ground provisions', consist of carrots (tough and woody, new carrots are rare), cassava, yams, eddoes, tannia and two kinds of potato, sweet and English (or Irish) potatoes. Ask simply for potatoes and one is given the sweet variety, therefore, all through this book the term English potatoes is used for the unsweet kind.

Above ground are globe artichokes, aubergines, (always called egg plant or garden eggs), cristophenes, also known as chocho and not to be confused with coco (another name for eddoe) and pumpkin which is often called by the American name, squash. Cabbages and cauliflower are expensive. Callaloo, the leaf of the eddoe, which tastes like spinach but looks different with much larger leaves, and various kinds of peas and beans complete the green vegetable list, and for salads there are lettuce, cucumber, tomatoes (rough and pale) and avocado pears which are always called simply *pears*.

Among tree vegetables are ackee, found mainly in Jamaica, breadfruit, bluggoes (cooking bananas), plantains and green pawpaw.

Women in the markets have piles of muddy, rough looking roots in their baskets and these are cassava, yams and sweet potatoes, the main source of edible starch; others offer 'seasonings', bunches of chives, parsley, thyme and sage and they usually have peppers and chillis (sweet and hot peppers as they are known). One gains the impression these market vendors cannot live off the few cents their produce brings in, but they come to be *in* the market, to join in haggling and jokes and to sleep in the shade at mid-day, head pillowed on a large melon or a pile of yams.

Saturday is the busy day, from Nassau, where out-island boats discharge at the quayside, down through Jamaica where Linstead, Papine and the colourful Cross Roads markets will be in full swing. In the U.S. Virgins, boats bring produce from the British Virgin Islands and near St. John's, Antigua, is an old covered market. Roseau market, in Dominica, muddy and steep, has the finest produce of all, for here, so they say, the soil is so rich a root pushed into the ground is a tree within a year. Continuing down the Eastern Caribbean to St. Vincent, famous for arrowroot, one comes to St. Lucia where the market is by Castries waterfront and the vendors can be heard shouting their patois, half French, half English and hard to understand. In the French islands, market scenes are even more colourful, dresses gayer and tighter with *foulards* worn knotted high. Grenada's market place, the centre of old rooftops in St. George's, is like an English country town; Barbados has a big market at the end of Bridgetown's main street. In Speightstown, women call their wares under the seaside trees . . . and so it goes on through the islands; the source of income for part of the population stems from the vegetable basket.

ACKEE SOUFFLE

Preparation time 10 minutes
Cooking time   25 – 30 minutes
Oven temperature 375°F., Gas Mark 5
To serve   4

You will need

1½ oz. butter
1½ oz. flour
½ pint (U.S. 1¼ cups) hot milk
3 eggs, separated
½ pint (U.S. 1¼ cups) ackee purée
1 teaspoon salt
½ teaspoon pepper
dash Worcestershire sauce

Butter a 1½-pint soufflé dish and tie a strip of butter-ed greaseproof paper round the outside to rise 2-inches above the top of the dish. Melt the butter in a saucepan, stir in the flour and add the milk very slowly, stirring all the time until the mixture is boiling. Allow to cool slightly, then beat in the egg yolks. Add the ackee and season with salt, pepper and Worcestershire sauce. Whisk the egg whites very stiffly and fold them lightly into the soufflé mixture. Turn into the prepared dish and bake immediately in a moderately hot oven for 25-30 minutes or until the soufflé is risen and very lightly browned.

Jamaican ackees

AUBERGINES BAKED WITH COCONUT CREAM
(Illustrated in colour on page 76)

Preparation time 8 minutes
Cooking time   50 minutes
Oven temperature 350°F., Gas Mark 4
To serve   4

You will need

2 small or 1 large aubergine, peeled and thinly
    sliced
3 onions, thinly sliced
salt and pepper
¾ pint (U.S. 2 cups) coconut cream (see page
    30)
1 small red chilli, de-seeded and very finely
    chopped

Lay the aubergine slices in a shallow casserole, spread with onion rings and sprinkle with a little salt and pepper. Pour over coconut cream and sprinkle with chopped chilli. Cover and bake in a moderate oven for 45 minutes. Remove cover and bake for a further 5 minutes.

BAKED AUBERGINE

Preparation time 6 – 8 minutes
Cooking time   2½ – 3 hours
Oven temperature 275°F., Gas Mark 1
To serve   4 – 5

You will need

3 small onions, thinly sliced
2 small or 1 large aubergine, peeled and thinly
    sliced
2 tomatoes, thinly sliced
salt and pepper
2 tablespoons vegetable oil

Arrange the vegetables in layers in a shallow casserole, starting and finishing with a layer of onion. Season each layer with a little salt and pepper, pour the oil over and bake in a very slow oven for 2½-3 hours, basting frequently with oil. Allow to cool, chill and serve very cold.

CREAMED BREADFRUIT

Cooking time for breadfruit depends largely on their size and whether or not they are ripe. Once cooked, they taste very much like English potatoes. They are delicious boiled, peeled, sliced, buttered and toasted under a hot grill and served like buttered toast.

Preparation time 5 – 7 minutes
Cooking time 40 – 50 minutes
Oven temperature 425°F., Gas Mark 7 (see method below)
To serve 4

You will need

1 ripe breadfruit
salt
½ oz. butter
pepper
¼ pint (U.S. ⅔ cup) hot milk
1 egg, separated (see method below)
deep fat or oil for frying (see method below)

Cook the breadfruit in boiling salted water for about 40 minutes, or until tender. Peel, core and mash, add the butter and season with salt and pepper. Add the milk slowly until the mixture is creamy but still stiff. At this stage it can be served (like mashed English potato).
A lighter mixture results by beating in the egg yolk and quickly folding in the whisked white. Pile into a greased pie dish and bake in a hot oven for about 10 minutes until golden brown on top. If preferred, the mixture can be piled in individual cones on a greased baking sheet or dropped from a spoon into hot fat or oil and fried.

SLICED BREADFRUIT

Preparation time 5 – 7 minutes
Cooking time about 50 minutes
To serve 4

You will need

1 ripe breadfruit
salt
3 rashers bacon
1 onion, sliced
pepper
¼ pint (U.S. ⅔ cup) stock (see page 21)
¼ pint (U.S. ⅔ cup) vinegar

Cook the breadfruit in boiling salted water until tender, about 40 minutes. Peel and slice while still hot. Remove rind from bacon, dice and fry until golden. Add the onion rings and fry until transparent. Season with salt and pepper, add the stock and vinegar and cook for a further 2 minutes. Pour over the hot sliced breadfruit and serve very hot.

FRIED BREADFRUIT

Preparation time 7 minutes
Cooking time 20 – 25 minutes
To serve 4

You will need

1 slightly under-ripe breadfruit
salt and pepper
1 teaspoon chopped chives (optional)
deep fat or oil for frying

Parboil the breadfruit for 15 minutes in boiling salted water. Peel, core and cut into about 8 slices. Sprinkle with salt, pepper and chives, if liked. Heat fat or oil and quickly fry breadfruit slices until golden.

STUFFED BREADFRUIT

Preparation time 10 minutes
Cooking time 1 hour
Oven temperature 375°F., Gas Mark 5
To serve 4

You will need

1 firm breadfruit
salt
½ oz. butter
8 oz. minced raw beef
8 oz. minced raw salt pork or ham
1 tomato, peeled, de-seeded and chopped
1 onion, chopped
pepper

Cook the breadfruit for 15 minutes in boiling salted water. Meanwhile heat the butter (use a little extra butter if the pork or ham is very lean) and fry the minced meat. Add the tomato and onion, season with salt and pepper and toss with a fork to blend well.

Slice off the stem end of the breadfruit thinly and retain the stem. Remove core, leaving a thick wall of fruit and stuff the cavity with the meat mixture. Replace the stems, skewering with cocktail sticks or plug the hole with foil. Bake on a greased tin in a moderately hot oven for about 45 minutes.

YOUNG BARBADOS CABBAGE

Cabbage is very expensive in the islands, especially in Barbados, where the locally grown type is tender and worthy of something a little better than boiling.

Preparation time 5 minutes
Cooking time about 30 minutes
To serve 4 – 6

You will need

1 firm cabbage
salt
about 2 oz. butter
pepper

Cook the cabbage, left whole, in lightly salted boiling water for about 20 minutes until nearly cooked. Drain and shake well to remove excess water. With a sharp knife, divide into quarters, cutting through nearly to the stalk. Fill the cuts with knobs of butter, sprinkle with pepper and simmer, tightly covered, for a further 10-15 minutes according to the size and tenderness of the cabbage, basting about three times with the melted butter.

CREAMED CALLALOO

Callaloo tastes very like spinach, which can be substituted for any callaloo dish, but it does not contain the water found in spinach; whereas spinach can cook in its own liquid, callaloo requires water.

Preparation time 10 minutes
Cooking time 40 – 45 minutes
To serve 4 – 5

You will need

16 – 18 callaloo leaves
1½ pints (U.S. 3¾ cups) boiling water
1½ oz. butter
2 tablespoons olive oil
1 onion, finely chopped
3 tablespoons single cream
1 oz. soft breadcrumbs
1 oz. cheese, grated
salt and pepper
pinch grated nutmeg

Wash the callaloo, chop the stems and remove the vein from the centre of each leaf. Put in a saucepan, pour over the boiling water (this is important because it keeps them a good colour) bring to the boil and simmer for about 35 minutes or until tender. Drain and rub through a sieve.
While the callaloo is cooking, heat the butter and oil in a frying pan and cook the onion until transparent. Add the onion mixture to the sieved callaloo and when the butter and oil are absorbed, add the cream, breadcrumbs, cheese, salt, pepper and nutmeg. Heat, but do not allow the mixture to boil.
Note
White sauce may replace the cream.

VARIATION
CALLALOO PUREE
Prepare exactly as above, stirring only butter into the callaloo when sieved. Season as for the creamed recipe.

Creamed callaloo

73

CALLALOO WITH CRAB

Preparation time 10 – 12 minutes
Cooking time 50 minutes
To serve 4

You will need

12 callaloo leaves
2 crabs
6 okras, cut into rings
1 onion, chopped
1 clove garlic, chopped
1 sprig thyme
salt
1½ pints (U.S. 3¾ cups) boiling water
pepper
dash Tabasco sauce
½ oz. butter

Wash the callaloo, chop the stems and remove the vein from the centre of each leaf. Scrub the crabs and scald in boiling water. Put callaloo, crabs, okras, onion, garlic, thyme and salt into a thick saucepan. Pour on the boiling water and simmer for 45 minutes. Drain off the liquid, discard the thyme, remove the crabs and pick out the meat. Return crab meat to the pot, season with pepper and Tabasco, swirl in the butter and serve very hot.

BAKED CRISTOPHENE

Cristophenes are pear-shaped, about the size of small melons and delicately green. They can be cooked like marrow and served with a white sauce. Marrows are there too, but with very pale, smooth green skins, unflecked and quite unlike European marrows in appearance, but tasting very much the same.

Preparation time 10 minutes
Cooking time 50 minutes
Oven temperature 400°F., Gas Mark 6
To serve 4

You will need

2 large cristophenes
½ oz. butter
1 onion, finely chopped
4 oz. minced raw beef
salt and pepper
1 oz. crisp breadcrumbs (raspings)
1 oz. cheese, grated

Parboil the cristophenes in boiling water for about 20 minutes, until they become a little soft. Cut them in half lengthways, scoop out the pulp leaving the shells intact. Chop and mash the half-cooked pulp. While the cristophenes are boiling, heat the butter and cook the onion until transparent. Add the meat, mix well and season to taste with salt and pepper. Simmer over a low heat for about 15 minutes or until the meat is cooked through. Blend in the cristophene pulp, season a little more if required and simmer for a further 2 minutes. Pile the mixture back into the shells and top with breadcrumbs and grated cheese. Put on a greased baking sheet and bake in a moderately hot oven for about 20 minutes, until delicately browned.

CUCUMBER WITH BACON
(Illustrated in colour on page 75)

Island cucumbers have little flavour and are rather rough outside, but very suitable for cooking.

Preparation time 10 minutes, plus 30 minutes draining
Cooking time 15 minutes
To serve 4 – 5

You will need

3 large or 4 medium-sized cucumbers, cut in ¼-inch slices
salt
4 rashers bacon
1 egg, beaten
soft breadcrumbs
2 oz. butter

Sprinkle cucumbers liberally with salt and set aside for 30 minutes to drain. Remove rind from bacon, cut into pieces and fry slowly until crisp, remove from pan and keep hot. Drain and dry cucumbers, dip in egg and toss in breadcrumbs. Heat butter with bacon fat remaining in pan and fry cucumbers until golden. Stir in bacon and serve hot.

Cucumber with bacon

Aubergines baked with coconut cream

Baked pumpkin

Avocado mould

EDDO PUDDING

Preparation time 10 minutes
Cooking time about 1 hour
Oven temperature 350°F., Gas Mark 4
To serve 4

You will need

4 eddoes
1 oz. butter
¼ pint (U.S. ⅔ cup) milk
½ teaspoon pepper
1 teaspoon salt
2 eggs, separated

Cook the eddoes in their skins in boiling water until tender, about 30 minutes. Slice off the tops and squeeze out the soft pulp. Mix with the butter, milk, pepper and salt and the lightly beaten egg yolks. Blend and beat a little. Whisk the egg whites very stiffly, fold into the eddo mixture and pour into a buttered dish, filling it about three-quarters full. Bake in a moderate oven for 25-30 minutes until the pudding has risen to the top of the dish. Serve at once.
Note
This dish can be served as a supper dish or as a vegetable. Potatoes, sweet or English, can be used in place of eddoes.

EDDOES WITH CREAM SAUCE

Preparation time 6 minutes
Cooking time 30 minutes
To serve 4

You will need

5 eddoes
salt
½ oz. butter
1 onion, finely chopped
1 small chilli, de-seeded and chopped
squeeze lime juice
dash Angostura Bitters

Cook the eddoes in their skins in boiling salted water until tender, about 30 minutes. Slice off the tops and squeeze out the pulp. While the eddoes are cooking, heat the butter in another saucepan, add the onion

and chilli and cook for 5 minutes. Stir in lime juice and cook for a further 2 minutes, add Angostura and pour over the pulped eddoes.

STEWED OKRA

Preparation time 5 minutes
Cooking time 35 minutes
To serve 4

You will need

1 oz. butter
1 onion, sliced
12 okras, cut in rings
2 tomatoes, chopped
salt and pepper
dash Tabasco sauce

Heat the butter in a frying pan and brown the onion and okra rings, stirring all the time. Add the tomato, season with salt and pepper and continue cooking over a low heat for about 30 minutes, stirring all the time until the vegetables are tender and the mixture thickens. Stir in the Tabasco just before serving.

FRIED OKRA

In the islands, fried or stewed okras would be eaten with rice as a meal. Choose only small, young okras for frying; the Caribbean kind are tough and rough skinned when large.

Preparation time 6 minutes
Cooking time 5 – 8 minutes
To serve 4

You will need

12 okras, cut in half lengthways
1 egg, lightly beaten
crisp breadcrumbs (raspings)
salt and pepper
fat or oil for frying

Dip okras in egg and roll in breadcrumbs seasoned with salt and pepper. Fry quickly in hot, shallow fat or oil. Drain and serve very hot.

GLOBE ARTICHOKES

Preparation time 15 minutes
Cooking time 20 minutes
To serve 4

You will need

4 artichokes
1 lime
1 – 1½ pints (U.S. 2½ – 3¾ cups) water
1 teaspoon salt
1 tablespoon vinegar or squeeze of lime juice

Cut off the stalk, trim the base and strip the tough outer leaves from each artichoke. Remove the inner 'choke' and snip the tips off the remaining leaves. Rub the base and outer leaves with cut lime, then tie round with thread to keep them tight while cooking. Bring the water to the boil, add salt and vinegar or lime juice. Gently put in the artichokes and boil for about 20 minutes, or until the base is soft. Drain thoroughly and allow them to dry, then serve with melted butter.

Herb fried onion

HERB FRIED ONION

A recipe from Bermuda, famous for its onion crop.

Preparation time 6 – 8 minutes
Cooking time 12 – 15 minutes
To serve 4

You will need

1½ oz. butter
3 tablespoons olive oil
3 onions, thickly sliced
2 teaspoons chopped marjoram
1 teaspoon chopped thyme
salt
cayenne pepper

Heat the butter in a thick frying pan, add the oil and when very hot, but not smoking, toss in the onion rings. Add the herbs, and season with a little salt and a good dash of cayenne. Stir until the onion is well coated with fat, then cover and cook over a low heat until just beginning to turn golden. Brown for 1 minute over a high heat.

BAKED GREEN PAWPAW

Preparation time 10 minutes
Cooking time 50 minutes
Oven temperature 400°F., Gas Mark 6
To serve 4

You will need

1 medium-sized green pawpaw
1 onion, chopped
2 teaspoons chopped chives
1½ oz. butter
salt and pepper
1 oz. crisp breadcrumbs (raspings)

Cook the pawpaw in boiling water for 30 minutes. Drain and cut in half lengthways. Remove the seeds and scoop out the pulp. Cook the onion and chives in 1 oz. of the butter. Mix with the pawpaw pulp and season with salt and pepper to taste. Pile back into the empty skins, sprinkle with breadcrumbs and dot with remaining butter. Bake for 20 minutes in a moderately hot oven until delicately browned.
Note
A little chopped tomato can be added to the mixture which can be cooked by itself without the additional vegetables, but cooked pawpaw is somewhat tasteless, something like marrow (which can be substituted), and is better with extra seasoning.

Curried green bananas or plantains

CURRIED GREEN BANANAS OR PLANTAINS

Visitors may confuse plantains with bananas; their appearance is much the same, but they are larger and cannot be eaten raw. Another use for plantains is conquintay flour, made from plantains, peeled and sliced lengthways and dried on a board in the hot sunshine. After about 5 days, when the strips are dry, they are pounded and sieved.

Preparation time 5 minutes
Cooking time 35 minutes
To serve 4 – 5

You will need

1½ oz. butter
1 tablespoon curry powder
6 green bananas or plantains, peeled and sliced lengthways
1 teaspoon salt
1 teaspoon pepper
¾ pint (U.S. 2 cups) coconut milk
1 egg, lightly beaten

Heat the butter, fry the curry powder for 2 minutes, then add the banana or plantain slices and brown lightly. Add salt and pepper and then the coconut milk, stirring with each addition. Simmer over a low heat for 30 minutes, remove from heat and stir in the egg. Serve with any rice dish or with plain boiled rice.

MASHED GREEN BANANAS OR PLANTAINS

Preparation time 5 minutes
Cooking time 30 – 35 minutes
To serve 4

You will need

6 green bananas or plantains, peeled and halved
¼ pint (U.S. ⅔ cup) wine vinegar
¼ pint (U.S. ⅔ cup) strained lime juice
pinch salt
1 oz. butter, melted
1 tablespoon flour
good pinch grated nutmeg
½ teaspoon powdered cinnamon
pinch cayenne pepper

Put the bananas or plantains in a saucepan with the vinegar and lime juice, bring to the boil, add the salt and simmer, covered, over a low heat for 25 minutes or until tender. Mash thoroughly. Blend the butter with the flour, nutmeg, cinnamon and cayenne, stir slowly into the banana mixture and cook for a further 3 minutes.

CANDIED SWEET POTATOES

Preparation time 10 minutes
Cooking time 30 – 35 minutes
To serve 4

You will need

4 medium-sized sweet potatoes
1 lb. dark brown sugar
generous ¼ pint (U.S. ¾ cup) water
1 oz. butter
strained juice 1 lime
pinch grated nutmeg
pinch powdered allspice

Cook potatoes in boiling water for about 20-30 minutes, drain, peel and slice them. Mix the sugar with the water, stir and add the butter, lime juice, nutmeg and allspice. Bring to the boil, stirring until the syrup begins to thicken. Add the potato slices and cook for a further 5 minutes.

Sweet potatoes baked in oranges

SWEET POTATOES BAKED IN ORANGES

Preparation time 10 minutes
Cooking time 50 minutes
Oven temperature 350°F., Gas Mark 4
To serve 4

You will need

4 – 5 sweet potatoes
5 large oranges
4 tablespoons single cream or top of milk
1 oz. butter
1 oz. castor sugar
pinch salt
parsley

Cook the potatoes in boiling water for 30 minutes until tender, drain, peel and mash. Slice the tops off 4 of the oranges and scoop out the flesh without breaking the shells. Cut the peel from the tops into thin strips for decoration. Squeeze the juice from the pulp and grate the rind of the 5th orange. Add cream, butter, sugar and salt to the mashed potatoes and beat the mixture well until blended. Beat in 4 tablespoons orange juice and the grated rind. Pipe or spoon into the orange shells and bake in a moderate oven for about 20 minutes, until browned on top. Put into a dish with orange strips and parsley.
Note
The above recipe may be used with English potatoes but will require a little sugar.

CANDIED AND BAKED SWEET POTATOES

Preparation time 10 minutes
Cooking time 50 minutes
Oven temperature 350°F., Gas Mark 4
To serve 4

You will need

4 medium-sized sweet potatoes
finely grated rind 1 orange
3 tablespoons dark brown sugar
3 tablespoons hot water
1 oz. softened butter

Parboil the potatoes in boiling water for 15 minutes, drain, peel and slice them. Arrange slices of potato in a greased dish. Cook all the other ingredients together for 5 minutes over a low heat, stirring. Pour over the potato slices and bake in a moderate oven for 25-30 minutes, basting with the syrup.

BAKED PUMPKIN (SQUASH)
(Illustrated in colour on page 77)

Pumpkin is very plentiful in the Caribbean and there are many types. Some are only small melon size and others are long and marrow shaped.

Preparation time 3 minutes
Cooking time about 50 minutes
Oven temperature 375°F., Gas Mark 5
To serve 4

You will need

1 small pumpkin, or a piece weighing about
   2 – 2½ lb.
1 oz. butter
salt and pepper

Divide the pumpkin into quarters or wedges and remove seeds. Dot with butter, season, place on a greased baking sheet and bake for about 50 minutes in a moderately hot oven. Baste with butter from time to time until pumpkin is tender.

PUMPKIN PUREE

Preparation time 5 – 6 minutes
Cooking time 25 minutes
To serve 4

You will need

2 – 2½ lb. peeled pumpkin, thinly sliced
6 eschalots or spring onions, thinly sliced
1 tablespoon water (optional)
salt and pepper
pinch grated nutmeg
½ oz. butter
1 tablespoon double cream
paprika

Put half the slices in the bottom of a saucepan. Put the eschalot or spring onion slices on top and cover with the remaining pumpkin. Cover the saucepan, putting a clean cloth under the lid to make a tighter fit and cook for 5 minutes over a moderate heat, shaking all the time to prevent sticking. The water can be added at this stage if necessary. Reduce the heat and cook for a further 20 minutes until vegetables are tender. Mash well, blend in salt, pepper, nutmeg and butter. Heat through again and stir in the cream just before serving, sprinkled with paprika.

Yam, sweet potato and eddoe

STUFFED PUMPKIN

Preparation time 10 minutes
Cooking time 15 minutes
Oven temperature 425°F., Gas Mark 7
To serve 4

You will need

4 wedges baked pumpkin (see opposite)
1 oz. butter
1 egg yolk, lightly beaten
salt and pepper
1 tablespoon double cream
4 tablespoons meat stuffing as for stuffed bread-
    fruit (see page 72) or baked cristophene
    (see page 74)

Scoop the cooked pumpkin from the shells and mash well with the butter, egg yolk, salt and pepper. Stir in the cream and press back to line the shells. Fill the centre of each wedge with meat stuffing and bake in a hot oven for 15 minutes.

BAKED TANNIA

Preparation time 5 minutes
Cooking time 1¼ hours
Oven temperature 400°F., Gas Mark 6
To serve 4

You will need

4 medium-sized tannias
2 tablespoons finely chopped parsley
1 tablespoon finely chopped chives
strained juice 1 lime
1 oz. butter
salt

Wash the tannias and bake in their skins for 1¼ hours in a moderately hot oven. Cut in half, sprinkle with parsley and chives and a liberal amount of strained lime juice. Put a pat of butter on each and season to taste with salt.
Note
There is really no substitute for tannia, but English potatoes, baked in their skins, are pleasant if given the same treatment.

TANNIA CAKES

Preparation time 5 minutes
Cooking time   about 15 minutes
To serve   4 – 6

You will need

4 tannias
1 tablespoon flour
½ teaspoon baking powder
1 teaspoon chopped chives
1 teaspoon chopped parsley
1 egg, lightly beaten
salt and pepper
deep fat or oil for frying

Boil tannias for 10 minutes, cool slightly then peel and grate. Mix all the other ingredients together, then add the grated tannia, beating it into the mixture. Heat the fat or oil, drop in the tannia mixture by the spoonful and fry until golden brown. Drain and serve very hot.

BAKED YAMS

Preparation time   15 minutes
Cooking time   1 hour 5 minutes
Oven temperatures 400°F., Gas Mark 6
                     then
                     350°F., Gas Mark 5
To serve   4 – 5

You will need

3 large yams
flour
salt
1½ oz. butter
about 3 tablespoons milk
pepper

Peel the yams and cut into halves or quarters. Mix the flour with a good pinch of salt and roll the yam pieces in this to coat them. Put on a baking sheet and bake in a moderately hot oven for about 45 minutes, or until soft inside when tested with a skewer. Reduce oven temperature to moderate and when yam pieces are cool enough to handle, thinly slice off one side of each piece. Scoop the soft cooked yam from the hard baked shell and mash it with most of the butter and enough milk to make it soft. Season with pepper and a little

Baked yams

more salt if liked and beat well. Roll the hard baked skins into a good shape and fill with the mashed mixture. Mark with a fork, brush with a little melted butter and return to the oven. Bake for a further 20 minutes in a moderate oven until delicately brown. Serve with crisply fried bacon.

SURINAM CURRIED SALAD

Preparation time   10 minutes
To serve   4

You will need

2 teaspoons curry powder
1 teaspoon wine vinegar
3 tablespoons cold cooked rice
scant ½ pint (U.S. 1 cup) mayonnaise (see
   page 88)
4 oz. cold veal, cut in ½-inch cubes
4 hard-boiled eggs, sliced
4 small tomatoes, sliced
1 cooked cristophene, peeled and cut into
   ¾-inch cubes

Mix the curry powder, vinegar and rice with the mayonnaise.
Pile the veal in the centre of a dish, surround with sliced egg and tomato and diced cristophene. Cover with the curry mayonnaise mixture.

MIXED VEGETABLE PLATTER

Preparation time 10 minutes
Cooking time 30 minutes
To serve 4

You will need

1 medium-sized cabbage, shredded
1 lb. string beans, sliced diagonally
1 cucumber, sliced
1 aubergine, sliced
1½ pints (U.S. 3¾ cups) salted water
2 tomatoes, quartered
1 hard-boiled egg, quartered

Cook cabbage, beans, cucumber and aubergine in the salted water for 30 minutes or until all are tender. Put a plate over the pan of boiling vegetables and lay the tomato and egg quarters on this to heat during the last 10 minutes. Arrange the well drained, cooked vegetables on a heated platter with the tomato and egg quarters and serve hot or cold with Peanut Sauce (see page 28).

Note
A little cayenne pepper may be sprinkled on to the vegetables but there is no added salt as this is an Indonesian dish. It is known locally as 'gado-gado'.

PORT-AU-PRINCE SALAD

Preparation time 10 minutes
To serve 4

You will need

1 crisp lettuce heart
1 green pepper, de-seeded and cut in rings
2 sticks celery, chopped
6 small eschalots or spring onions
2 small carrots, peeled and finely diced
½ cooked breadfruit, peeled and diced
3 slices bread, cut into ½-inch cubes and fried in garlic flavoured butter
¼ pint (U.S. ⅔ cup) French dressing (see page 89)
1 avocado pear
strained juice 1 lime

Arrange lettuce leaves on a plate. Cut pepper rings in half, reserving one ring for garnish. Mix together celery, eschalots or spring onions, pepper, carrots, breadfruit and garlic bread cubes. Pile on top of lettuce and pour over the French dressing slowly, tossing well. Just before serving, peel avocado, remove stone and cut into wedges. Sprinkle with lime juice and arrange on top of salad with pepper ring.

Mixed vegetable platter

Port-au-Prince salad

85

FISH AND CRISTOPHENE VINAIGRETTE

Preparation time 15 minutes, plus chilling time
Cooking time 10 minutes
To serve 4

You will need

1 large cristophene
1 tablespoon strained lime juice
1 small onion, grated
1 teaspoon chopped thyme
¼ teaspoon dry mustard
pinch salt
pinch cayenne pepper
3 tablespoons olive oil
about 12 oz. cooked fish, flaked

Boil the cristophene for 10 minutes. Allow to cool, then chill. Put all the other ingredients except the fish into a small bowl, stand in a larger bowl filled with ice and beat lightly. When well blended, peel and grate the cristophene and stir into the mixture. Arrange the fish to cover the bottom of a shallow, chilled dish and put the cristophene mixture on top.

AVOCADO MOULD

(Illustrated in colour on page 78)

Preparation time 15 minutes
To serve 4 – 6

You will need

½ oz. packet powdered gelatine
3 tablespoons cold water
½ pint (U.S. 1¼ cups) boiling water
1 teaspoon castor sugar
4 avocado pears
¼ pint (U.S. ⅔ cup) mayonnaise (see page 88)
strained juice 1 lime
4 tablespoons single cream
½ teaspoon salt
pinch pepper
pinch cayenne pepper

TO GARNISH
1 avocado pear
1 tablespoon strained lime juice

Soften the gelatine in cold water, add the boiling water and stir in a bowl over a pan of boiling water until dissolved. Stir in the sugar. Cool until it begins to set. Peel avocado pears, remove stones, mash to a pulp and blend with mayonnaise, lime juice and cream. Season with salt, pepper and cayenne and add the cooled gelatine mixture blending thoroughly. Oil a loaf tin or mould and fill with the mixture, refrigerate until firmly set. Turn out mould.

TO GARNISH

Peel avocado, remove stone, cut into slices, sprinkle with lime juice and pile on top of the mould.

RED PEA AND FLYING FISH SALAD

Preparation time 15 minutes, plus overnight soaking and chilling
Cooking time 20 minutes
To serve 4

You will need

4 oz. red 'peas' (kidney beans)
salt
2 cooked flying fish, flaked
3 teaspoons finely chopped parsley
2 teaspoons finely chopped chives
1 onion, minced
1 small green pepper, de-seeded and chopped
¼ pint (U.S. ⅔ cup) French dressing (see page 89)
1 small firm cabbage, shredded
¼ pint (U.S. ⅔ cup) mayonnaise (see page 88)

TO GARNISH
2 small tomatoes, sliced
2 hard-boiled eggs, sliced
cayenne pepper

Soak peas in salt water overnight. Cook in water in which they soaked for 20 minutes or until tender, but not too soft. Drain and mix with fish. Add half the parsley and chives, the onion and pepper. Pour over French dressing, toss lightly and chill. Arrange shredded cabbage in a salad bowl, drain pea and flying fish mixture and pile on top. Coat with mayonnaise, thinned if necessary with a little of the drained French dressing. Garnish with tomato and egg slices, sprinkle with remaining parsley and chives and cayenne pepper.

Onion and orange salad

ONION AND ORANGE SALAD

Preparation time 8 minutes
To serve 4

You will need

3 oranges
2 onions, finely sliced
strained juice 1 small lime
2 teaspoons finely chopped marjoram
3 tablespoons olive oil
salt and pepper

Squeeze the juice from one orange. Peel the remaining oranges, including all the white pith and cut into pieces, discarding pips. Mix orange pieces with onion and marjoram and arrange on individual salad plates or in a glass dish. Mix lime and orange juice and blend with the oil. Add seasoning and pour over the salad. This is a very good salad to serve with cold duck or game.

SALAD 'FOREVER SPRING'

Preparation time 10 minutes
To serve 4

You will need

2 crisp lettuce hearts, halved
4 slices pineapple, peeled and the centres removed
4 tablespoons double cream or cottage cheese
4 bananas, peeled and sliced
2 grapefruit
pepper
4 tablespoons mayonnaise (see page 88)
2 tablespoons single cream
2 oz. blanched peanuts, finely chopped

Arrange the lettuce hearts on individual salad plates, flattening to a nice shape showing the heart. Slash the pineapple slices in six or eight places, open out to a flower shape, and place on top of lettuce. Fill the centre hole with double cream or cottage cheese and surround with overlapping banana slices. Peel grapefruit, including all the pith, divide into segments and discard the pips. Lay about four grapefruit segments on top of the bananas. Sprinkle with a little pepper and top with mayonnaise, thinned with single cream. Sprinkle with chopped nuts.

BREADFRUIT SALAD

Preparation time 8 – 10 minutes
To serve 4

You will need

2 hard-boiled eggs
2 teaspoons made mustard
$\frac{1}{2}$ oz. butter, melted
3 tablespoons single cream
dash Worcestershire sauce
salt and pepper
2 tablespoons wine vinegar
1 cooked breadfruit
1 onion, grated

Separate egg yolks from whites, and chop the whites. Mash yolks and mix with the mustard, butter, cream and Worcestershire sauce, then add the vinegar very slowly, stirring all the time. Peel, core and thinly slice the breadfruit and arrange the slices to cover the bottom of a salad dish, sprinkle with the egg white and onion and spread the egg yolk dressing over the top.
Note
Cold cooked English potato can be used in place of breadfruit.

Spiced island beetroot

SPICED ISLAND BEETROOT

Preparation time 6 minutes, plus standing time
Cooking time 1 – 1½ hours
Oven temperature 375°F., Gas Mark 5
To serve 4

You will need

4 – 5 small beetroots
about 4 tablespoons French dressing (see page 89)
1 clove garlic, crushed
1 onion, sliced
2 cloves
1 bay leaf
salt and pepper
dash cayenne pepper

Wash the beetroots thoroughly. Scrape lightly but leave the stems on to prevent bleeding. Place on a baking sheet and bake in a moderately hot oven for 1–1½ hours or until tender. When cool enough to handle, rub off the skins with the thumb and cut off the stems. When quite cool, thinly slice and set aside for about 30 minutes to drain. Mix the beetroot juice with an equal amount of French dressing, add garlic, onion, cloves, bay leaf, salt, pepper and cayenne. Refrigerate overnight, then strain. Arrange the sliced beetroot on individual salad plates with the onion and pour over the dressing.

CALABASH CHICKEN SHADDOCK SALAD

(Illustrated in colour on the frontispiece)

Preparation time 10 minutes, plus 20 minutes chilling
To serve 4

You will need

1 shaddock
1 lb. cooked chicken, diced
1 green pepper, de-seeded and sliced
½ cucumber, cut in small pieces
2 tomatoes, quartered
¼ pint (U.S. ⅔ cup) French dressing (see page 89)
¼ pint (U.S. ⅔ cup) mayonnaise (see page 88)
½ teaspoon curry powder
1 small onion, grated
1 teaspoon chopped chives
2 teaspoons chopped parsley
1 lettuce

Peel shaddock, removing all the white pith, cut into segments and discard pips.
Toss the chicken, pepper, cucumber, shaddock and tomatoes in French dressing and chill for 20 minutes. Blend the mayonnaise with curry powder, onion, chives and parsley. Line individual salad bowls with crisp lettuce leaves. When chilled, drain the chicken mixture, toss in the mayonnaise and pile into the bowls.

VARIATION
Chopped ham can replace half the chicken.

MAYONNAISE

Preparation time 10 minutes
To make ½ pint

You will need

2 egg yolks
½ teaspoon salt
pinch white pepper
½ teaspoon dry mustard
2 teaspoons vinegar or strained lime juice
½ pint (U.S. 1¼ cups) olive oil

Warm a bowl and beat the egg yolks. Add salt, pepper, mustard and half the vinegar or lime juice. Mix well, then add the oil drop by drop, beating all the time, until a quarter of the quantity is used. Add half the remaining vinegar or lime juice and still beating, add the rest of the oil, stoping from time to time to make sure the mixture is well blended. When all the oil is used, add the last $\frac{1}{2}$ teaspoon of vinegar or lime juice. A blender may be used, but it must be set at medium to avoid overheating. If the mixture curdles, put an extra egg yolk in a clean bowl, wash the beater or blender and very slowly add the curdled mixture to the fresh egg yolk, beating all the time.

FRENCH DRESSING

Preparation time 5 minutes
To make 1 pint

You will need

$\frac{1}{2}$ teaspoon dry mustard
2 teaspoons salt
1 teaspoon pepper
$\frac{1}{4}$ teaspoon castor sugar
$\frac{1}{4}$ pint (U.S. $\frac{2}{3}$ cup) lime juice or white vinegar
$\frac{3}{4}$ pint (U.S. 2 cups) olive oil

Put all the ingredients in a screw-top jar, shake well and allow to stand for 5 minutes. In the tropics, it is necessary to store the dressing in the refrigerator, but it should be removed about 30 minutes before it is required as the oil thickens. In temperate climates, the dressing can be stored in a cool, dry place. If the dressing is not required for storing, make only half quantities.

ANGOSTURA CREAM

Preparation time 5 minutes
To make about $\frac{1}{4}$ pint

You will need

2 tablespoons made mustard
2 tablespoons vinegar
$\frac{1}{4}$ teaspoon salt
2 tablespoons castor sugar
2 tablespoons evaporated milk
1 tablespoon Angostura Bitters

Mix all the ingredients and beat with a rotary beater until fluffy.
Note
This is a very hot dressing, if a milder one is required, reduce the amount of mustard.

MOLASSES DRESSING

Preparation time 5 minutes, plus cooling time
Cooking time 4 minutes
To make about $\frac{1}{2}$ pint

You will need

8 oz. molasses
2 egg yolks, well beaten
salt and pepper
2 tablespoons strained lime juice
5 tablespoons double cream, lightly whipped
$\frac{1}{4}$ teaspoon powdered ginger

Heat molasses to boiling point and allow to cool a little. Slowly add the egg yolks and cook for 2 minutes over a very low heat, without boiling, stirring all the time and scraping the bottom of the pan. Cool, add a pinch of salt and pepper and then the lime juice. Fold in the cream with the ginger. This dressing is suitable for serving with salads which contain fruit such as grapefruit, shaddock and avocado.

Jamaican pineapple pie

DESSERTS

'Rum, coconuts and fruit, what better foundation for an array of attractive desserts? These are the 'naturals' of the Caribbean where the background of cane is the sweetest of all the products. Islanders, however, tend to prefer heavier puddings and use plenty of cornflour and gelatine, but some old family recipes are more subtle and a few small hotels have evolved their own delicate desserts from local fruit. Calabash, in Grenada, makes Sapodilla Delight which has an elusive flavour, like the Soursop Fool which I very often serve myself. Neither of these transport well, nor do they grow everywhere in the world; readers must visit the Caribbean to savour their strange, delicious flavour but both recipes can be used with other fruits as the base.

Guava cup tarts will look much the same if stewing pears are used for the filling; Pineapple Pie makes a change from the traditional apple pie of a British Sunday lunch; bananas aflame in rum can be produced anywhere and this dessert is almost certain to be offered to the Caribbean traveller within a few days of arrival. Coconut may have to be desiccated, but coconut cream can be served instead of dairy cream and rum is the perfect flavouring for many sophisticated sweets.

Pile on the dark brown sugar and you pile on the heart of the West Indies, the corner stone of island economy for centuries past. For me, the simple purchase of a packet of sugar in the city always brings back memories of 'crop', the February harvest time for cane. Memories of bent backs as women gather cut canes, of flying machettes as the stalks are skilfully cut, of that strange, crude smell of 'bagasse', waste from the sugar factories used again as fuel and fertiliser. Sounds of a rushing train always remind me of the grinding, which must be done as soon as the cane is cut down, any road, anywhere, will suddenly evoke memories of cane trucks, loaded high and the tiny donkey cart of some small farmer carrying his year's output to the sweet melting pot of the sugar industry.

BASIC FLAN PASTRY

Preparation time 10 minutes
To line   a 9-inch flan ring or tin

You will need

8 oz. plain flour
pinch salt
3 – 4 oz. butter
3 – 4 oz. cooking fat
iced water

Sift flour and salt into a chilled bowl. Using two knives, cut fat into the flour until it flakes, then add just enough water, 1 teaspoon at a time, to hold the pastry together. Blend the water in with a fork.
Note
In the tropics, it is very helpful to have a bowl of ice on the table to chill the hands and utensils as the pastry is made.

Burnt sugar pudding

BURNT SUGAR PUDDING

Making this dessert always reminds me of living among the cane fields where everyone knows what the cry 'Cane fire' means. As the fire engine's siren shrills, every window and door must be closed to keep out the thick layer of black dust.

Preparation time 10 minutes
Cooking time 35 – 40 minutes
Oven temperature 375° F., Gas Mark 5
To serve 4 – 5

You will need

8 oz. brown sugar
½ pint (U.S. 1¼ cups) boiling water
3 *thick* slices stale bread
pinch salt
½ teaspoon vanilla essence
¾ pint (U.S. 2 cups) hot milk
3 eggs, well beaten
good pinch grated nutmeg

In a thick saucepan, melt the sugar until very dark brown, then add the boiling water and simmer until the syrup is thick. Remove crusts from bread and cut into cubes. Butter a soufflé dish and arrange the bread cubes to cover the bottom. Add salt and vanilla to the hot milk and pour very slowly over the beaten eggs. Pour caramel over bread, add the milk and egg mixture and top with nutmeg. Stand soufflé dish in a pan of hot water and bake in a moderately hot oven for 30 minutes. Put under a hot grill for 3 minutes to brown the top of the pudding.

JAMAICAN PINEAPPLE PIE

The supply of pineapples varies from island to island, but they are usually plentiful in Jamaica, and Eleuthera, in the Bahamas is famous for its pines.

Preparation time 20 minutes, plus chilling time
Cooking time 45 minutes
Oven temperatures 425°F., Gas Mark 7
then
375°F., Gas Mark 5
To serve 6

You will need

12 oz. basic flan pastry (see page 91)

FOR THE FILLING
1 large pineapple, peeled and cut into chunks
8 oz. granulated sugar
1½ oz. flour
¼ teaspoon grated nutmeg
pinch powdered cinnamon
pinch salt
1½ oz. butter
2 tablespoons water (optional)

Roll out half the pastry and use to line the bottom of a pie dish. Chill. Roll out second half, 1-inch larger than the top of the pie dish and chill.

FOR THE FILLING
Mix pineapple, sugar, flour, nutmeg, cinnamon and salt. Cook over a low heat until the mixture thickens, then remove from the heat, stir in butter and the water if the mixture is very thick. Allow to cool.
Pour into the chilled pastry case. Cover with rolled-our pastry, neatly tucking under the overhang and sealing by damping the edges and pressing between finger and thumb. Make a slit in the top to allow the steam to escape. Flute edges. Bake in a hot oven for 10 minutes, then reduce oven to moderately hot and bake for a further 30 minutes until crust is delicately brown. Decorate with pineapple leaves in the centre and serve with coconut cream (see page 30) or soft cream cheese. Illustrated in black and white on page 90.
Note
Canned pineapple may be used for the filling.

GUAVA TART

Preparation time 15 minutes, plus chilling time
Cooking time 30 minutes
Oven temperature 425°F., Gas Mark 7
To serve 6

You will need

8 oz. basic flan pastry (see page 91)

FOR THE FILLING
10 – 12 ripe guavas, halved
½ pint (U.S. 1¼ cups) plus 2 tablespoons water
8 oz. granulated sugar
1 oz. cornflour
1 teaspoon vanilla essence
½ oz. butter

Roll out the pastry to a 10½-inch circle on a lightly floured board or marble slab. Lift into a 9-inch flan ring, placed on a baking sheet, or flan tin and trim edges. Prick base and chill. Fill the chilled flan case with greaseproof paper and rice and bake 'blind' in a hot oven for 10 minutes. Remove greaseproof paper and rice and bake for a further 5 minutes to dry out the base. Allow to cool.

FOR THE FILLING
Put the guava halves in a pan with ½ pint (U.S. 1¼ cups) water and simmer over a low heat for about 15 minutes, until soft, but not mushy. Remove from the heat and, when cool enough to handle, scoop out the pulp and slip off the skins, being careful to keep the shells intact. Return the pulp to the pan with the juice, add the sugar and simmer for a further 5 minutes, then remove from the heat and sieve. Mix the cornflour to a smooth paste with the 2 tablespoons water, add the vanilla and stir into the sieved guava pulp and juice. Cook, stirring, over a moderate heat until the mixture thickens, about 5 minutes. Remove from the heat and beat in the butter. Arrange the guava shells in the pastry case and pour over the thickened juice. Cool, chill and serve with coconut cream (see page 30) or dairy cream.

VARIATION
Individual pastry cases, each with one guava shell inside, make an attractive party dessert.
Note
Canned guavas or stewing pears can be used.

SPICED BANANAS

There are nearly always bananas on the islands, ripening very quickly once the 'hands' are cut. Banana cutting is a specialised job, the tree exudes a black latex substance which stains the workers clothes and sometimes the skin of the fruit. The worker knows the exact moment when the fruit is ripe and cuts down the whole tree. In the great plantations around Bowden at the South Eastern tip of Jamaica, almost every man, woman and child carries a machette with which to harvest the fruit. Bananas make the basis of several delicious desserts and are widely used throughout the islands of the Caribbean. These sweet yellow bananas which are a familiar sight in our green grocers should not be confused with the green bananas or plantains which are also popular in these islands but which are always cooked and used in savoury dishes.

Preparation time 10 minutes
Cooking time 15 minutes
Oven temperature 375°F., Gas Mark 5
To serve 4

You will need

4 firm bananas, peeled and quartered
2 teaspoons lime juice
1 oz. butter
pinch salt
½ pint (U.S. 1¼ cups) rum
6 oz. brown sugar
½ teaspoon grated nutmeg
½ teaspoon powdered cinnamon
¼ teaspoon powdered allspice
finely grated rind ½ orange
about 4 biscuits, finely crushed
about 12 blanched peanuts, finely chopped
2 sugar lumps

Sprinkle the banana quarters with lime juice. Heat the butter and brown them lightly, shaking the pan all the time. Sprinkle very sparingly with salt. Combine nearly all the rum, the sugar, nutmeg, cinnamon, allspice and orange rind. Place the bananas in a buttered dish, pour over the rum and spice mixture and top with a layer of biscuit crumbs mixed with chopped peanuts. Bake in a moderately hot oven for 12 minutes. Just before serving, put the sugar in a ladle with the remaining rum, set alight, pour over the pudding and serve flaming.

CORAL REEF COCONUT CREAM PIE

(Illustrated in colour on page 95)

Coral Reef is one of the nicest of the Barbados West coast hotels renowned for the buffet lunch desserts.

Preparation time	20 minutes, plus chilling time
Cooking time	1 hour
Oven temperatures	450°F., Gas Mark 8
	then
	375° F., Gas Mark 5
To serve	6

You will need

8 oz. basic flan pastry (see page 91)

FOR THE FILLING
2 oz. castor sugar
pinch salt
pinch grated nutmeg
4 oz. peeled ripe coconut, finely grated
1 teaspoon vanilla essence
½ pint (U.S. 1¼ cups) hot milk
3 egg yolks, lightly beaten

FOR THE TOPPING
3 egg whites
pinch cream of tartar
4 oz. castor sugar
½ teaspoon vanilla essence
glacé cherries

Roll out the pastry to a 10½-inch circle on a lightly floured board or marble slab. Lift into a 9-inch flan ring, placed on a baking sheet, or flan tin and trim edges. Prick base and chill.

FOR THE FILLING
Add sugar, salt, nutmeg, coconut and vanilla to the milk and stir in the egg yolks until well blended. Turn into the pastry case and bake immediately in a very hot oven for 10 minutes. Reduce heat to moderately hot to prevent filling curdling and continue baking for a further 35 minutes or until filling has set. Allow to cool.

FOR THE TOPPING
Beat the egg whites with cream of tartar until stiff and then add the sugar and vanilla very slowly, beating all the time. When the pie is cool, spread the meringue topping over the filling, taking it just over the edge of the pastry. Bake in a moderately hot oven for 12 – 15 minutes until lightly browned. Decorate with cherries and serve hot or cold.

BANANA RUM ICE PIE

Preparation time	15 minutes, plus chilling time
Cooking time	20 – 25 minutes
Oven temperatures	425°F., Gas Mark 7
	then
	450°F., Gas Mark 8
To serve	6

You will need

8 oz. basic flan pastry (see page 91)

FOR THE FILLING
banana rum ice cream, using 2 bananas (see page 99)
12 seedless raisins, soaked in rum to plump

FOR THE TOPPING
3 egg whites
pinch salt
pinch cream of tartar
4 oz. castor sugar
1 teaspoon vanilla essence

Roll out the pastry to a 10½-inch circle on a lightly floured board or marble slab. Lift into a 9-inch flan ring, placed on a baking sheet, or flan tin and trim edges. Prick base and chill. Fill the chilled flan case with greaseproof paper and rice and bake 'blind' in a hot oven for 10 minutes. Remove greaseproof paper and rice and bake for a further 5 minutes to dry out the base. Allow to cool.

FOR THE FILLING
Before freezing the ice cream, mix in the drained raisins, then freeze until very hard.

FOR THE TOPPING
Beat the egg whites with salt and cream of tartar until stiff, then add the sugar and vanilla very slowly, beating all the time.
Fill the pastry case with hard frozen ice cream and spread the meringue on top taking it just over the edge of the pastry. Bake immediately in a very hot oven for about 5 minutes or until the meringue is delicately browned.

Coral Reef coconut cream pie

Mango ice cream

BAKED LIME PUDDING

This is an old 'great house' recipe that was given to me at Lucea, on the North West coast of Jamaica. Lucea is the prettiest little town and harbour and, at the time of writing, one of the few unspoilt parts of the Jamaican North shore.

Preparation time 10 minutes
Cooking time 25 – 30 minutes
Oven temperature 375°F., Gas Mark 5
To serve 4 – 5

You will need

2 oz. castor sugar
1 oz. flour
½ teaspoon powdered cinnamon
pinch salt
2 whole eggs, separated
1 egg yolk
3 tablespoons rum
grated rind and strained juice 1 large or 2 small limes
½ pint (U.S. 1¼ cups) milk

Sift together sugar, flour, cinnamon and salt. Beat the egg yolks with the rum and lime rind and juice. Add the egg mixture alternately with the milk to the sugar and flour, stirring all the time until well blended. Beat egg whites very stiffly, fold into the mixture and pour into a buttered pie dish. Stand in a pan of hot water and bake in a moderately hot oven for 25–30 minutes.

SAPODILLA DELIGHT

Preparation time 8 – 10 minutes
To serve 4

You will need

5 sapodillas
½ pint (U.S. 1¼ cups) coconut cream (see page 30)
6 tablespoons evaporated milk
5 tablespoons sweetened condensed milk
1 tablespoon powdered gelatine
3 tablespoons boiling water

Scoop the pulp out of the skins, remove the sapodilla seeds, chop four roughly and slice the fifth fruit. Blend coconut cream and evaporated and con-densed milk. Beat well until frothy. Dissolve the gelatine in the boiling water, allow to cool slightly, then blend with the milk mixture, beating well. Stir in the chopped fruit, pour into individual soufflé dishes and decorate with the reserved fruit slices. Chill well before serving.

Note
Apricots or mangoes can be used in the same manner.

BUCCOO PAWPAW CUSTARD

Preparation time 10 – 12 minutes
Cooking time 30 minutes
Oven temperature 375°F., Gas Mark 5
To serve 4

You will need

1 large ripe pawpaw
10 oz. peeled ripe coconut, grated
¼ pint (U.S. ⅔ cup) double cream
generous ¼ pint (U.S. ¾ cup) milk
½ teaspoon vanilla essence
3 eggs, beaten
pinch salt
2 oz. castor sugar
1 orange

Scoop out flesh from pawpaw and sieve; the paw-paw should yield about 1 pint (U.S. 2½ cups) of purée. Mix with coconut. Butter a pie dish or pudding basin (if the dessert is to be served cold) and spread mixture over the bottom. Heat the cream with the milk and vanilla. Beat eggs with salt and sugar and still beating, pour on the milk mixture very slowly and beat until sugar is quite dissolved. Grate orange rind. Peel, removing all the white pith, cut out sections and chop, removing pips. Blend into egg mixture with rind and pour over the paw-paw. Place dish in a pan of hot water and bake in a moderately hot oven for 30 minutes, until custard sets. Serve hot in the pie dish, or loosen the edges, turn out on to a dish and chill. Serve with melted guava jelly (see page 113).

Note
Nothing can, of course, quite replace fresh pawpaw which is so abundant in the tropics, but canned pawpaw is obtainable in many big cities. Although the flavour is utterly different, this dessert is delicious made with apple purée with a squeeze of lemon juice and an extra tablespoon of sugar.

Banana bakes

BANANA BAKES

This is a very favourite way of cooking bananas in Jamaica; it is sometimes used for outdoor meals.

Preparation time 5 minutes
Cooking time   7 minutes
Oven temperature 425°F., Gas Mark 7
To serve   3

You will need

3 large bananas
2 teaspoons strained lime juice
1 tablespoon rum (optional)

Peel a thin strip from each banana and scoop out the fruit from the skins, keeping the skins intact. Mash bananas well, blending with the lime juice and rum, if liked. Replace inside the skins, marking the top with a criss-cross pattern. Bake in a hot oven for 7 minutes until delicately golden.

SOURSOP FOOL

Soursop grows in the West Indies and in South America and must be tasted there as it does not transport well. Superstition has it that the leaves placed around the head, have a soothing and soporific effect and also drive off 'duppies' or evil spirits!

Preparation time 7 minutes
To serve   4

You will need

1 large ripe soursop
basic vanilla ice cream, using 1 egg yolk (see page 98)

Halve the soursop and peel. Rub the pulp through a fine sieve, working it well to extract all the juice. Blend with ice cream, pile into sundae glasses and chill.
Note
The above is not the traditional recipe, which uses soursop with sugar and set with gelatine, but with such an extremely acid fruit, I find this makes a much milder and more palatable dessert.

BASIC VANILLA ICE CREAM

Preparation time 5 – 7 minutes, plus freezing time
Cooking time   7 minutes
To serve   6

You will need

3 egg yolks, well beaten
2 oz. castor sugar
pinch salt
¾ pint (U.S. 2 cups) single cream
scant ½ pint (U.S. 1 cup) double cream
1 teaspoon vanilla essence

Set the refrigerator at the coldest setting. Combine the beaten egg yolks with the sugar and salt, beating until the sugar dissolves. Heat the single cream in the top of a double saucepan and pour slowly on to the egg and sugar mixture. Strain back into the top of the double saucepan and cook until thickened. Chill, then blend the double cream with the vanilla and stir into the chilled mixture. Freeze. When half-frozen, remove from the refrigerator and stir. Return to the refrigerator and freeze until firm.
Note
Rich milk can be used in place of the single cream and I have used canned cream for the double cream with good results.

BANANA RUM ICE CREAM

Preparation time 8 – 10 minutes, plus freezing time
To serve 4

You will need

6 tablespoons rum
4 ripe bananas, peeled and mashed
pinch salt
1 egg white
generous ¼ pint (U.S. ¾ cup) single cream
generous ¼ pint (U.S. ¾ cup) milk

Set the refrigerator at the coldest setting. Blend the rum with the mashed bananas and add salt. Stiffly whisk the egg white and fold in. Stir in the cream and milk very slowly until well mixed; a blender, set at medium to avoid over-heating, is best for this. Pour the mixture into the freezing tray, remove from the refrigerator when half-frozen and stir once. Freeze until firm.
Note
All milk may be used instead of half milk and cream and about 12 raisins, soaked in rum to plump them, can be stirred into the half-frozen mixture.

ORANGE PEKOE ICE

Preparation time 7 minutes, plus 10 minutes steeping and freezing time
Cooking time 7 – 10 minutes
To serve 4

You will need

¼ pint (U.S. ⅔ cup) boiling water
1 tablespoon orange pekoe tea
4 oz. castor sugar
3 egg yolks, well beaten
finely grated rind 1 lime
½ pint (U.S. 1¼ cups) double cream, lightly whipped

Make sure the water is fast boiling, then make the tea. Cover the pot and steep for 10 minutes. While tea is steeping, blend sugar with beaten egg yolks, in the top of a double saucepan. Strain tea and add. Cook, stirring all the time, until thick and creamy. Pour the mixture into a clean bowl, stand on ice and stir until slightly cool, then chill. Fold the lime rind into the cream and stir into the cooled tea mixture. Pour into individual moulds and freeze. When half-frozen, remove from refrigerator and stir. Freeze until firm.

MANGO ICE CREAM

(Illustrated in colour on page 96)

Early mangoes are apt to be stringy but can be used very successfully for this ice. The number of mangoes depends very much on the type, if using Julies or Bombays, 3 may be enough.

Preparation time 10 minutes, plus freezing time
Cooking time 10 minutes
To serve 4 – 5

You will need

pinch cream of tartar
8 oz. castor sugar
4 tablespoons water
about 4 ripe mangoes
strained juice 1 lime
¾ pint (U.S. 2 cups) double cream, lightly whipped

Set refrigerator to coldest setting. Mix the cream of tartar and sugar with the water. Bring to the boil and cook over a low heat, stirring until the syrup thickens. Peel, remove stones, and sieve mangoes; the mangoes should yield about ½ pint (U.S. 1¼ cups) purée. Add mango purée to syrup with lime juice. Stir in cream until well blended. Turn into freezing tray and freeze. When half-frozen remove from refrigerator and stir. Freeze until firm.
Note
Soursop, rubbed through a sieve, makes a very good ice using this recipe, but the lime juice is not required as the fruit is rather acid. Away from the tropics, use ripe apricots or peaches in exactly the same way and, of course, lemon juice can always take the place of lime.

CAKES, BREADS AND COOKIES

For obvious reasons, pastries and cream cakes are unsuitable in the tropics; even with today's air-conditioning, elaborate gâteaux are not common in the islands. Local ladies love to make their squares of brightly iced sponge, but breads are the Caribbean *forte*. Cassava bread and cassava 'pone' are the staple breads of the islanders. Coconut, spice and banana bread are all delicious and Jamaican Gingerbread will be popular in every home. The rice cake (see opposite) and refrigerator cakes (see below) are equally suitable for a dessert for lunch or dinner as for tea.

Sometimes tea-time guests in the islands are given sorrel (see page 146) to drink just before they depart.

RUM COFFEE REFRIGERATOR CAKE

Preparation time 15 – 20 minutes

You will need

approximately 24 Savoy finger biscuits
2 tablespoons Tia Maria liqueur
4 oz. butter, softened
10 oz. icing sugar, sifted
2 egg yolks, beaten
3 oz. unsweetened chocolate
2 tablespoons triple strength black coffee
1 tablespoon rum
1 tablespoon strained orange juice
3 oz. blanched pecan or peanuts, chopped

Arrange the Savoy fingers to cover the sides and bottom of a 9-inch loaf tin, standing them edge to edge round the sides and cutting them to fit across the bottom. Crush the pieces left over and a few extra biscuits and mix to a paste with about 2 teaspoons Tia Maria. Use this to fill in any gaps in the biscuit wall.

Cream together butter and sugar and add the egg yolks. Melt the chocolate in the top of a double saucepan and beat into the egg mixture with the coffee, rum, orange juice and remaining liqueur. Mix well, then stir in the chopped nuts. Pour into the lined tin, smoothing off by pressing with a cut orange. Refrigerate until set, then with a sharp knife, cut off the tips of the biscuits so that they are level with the top of the filling.

Refrigerate or freeze, wrapped in foil, until required, then turn out.

REFRIGERATOR BISCUIT CAKE

Preparation time 10 – 12 minutes

You will need

8 oz. wholemeal biscuits
4 oz. unsweetened chocolate
2 tablespoons clear thick honey
2 oz. butter
2 oz. chopped blanched pecan or peanuts

Crush the biscuits between two clean sheets of paper. Brush an 8-inch sandwich tin with oil, greasing thoroughly but very lightly. Break up the chocolate and melt it in a small saucepan with the honey and butter; do not *cook*, only allow the ingredients to melt. Stir in the biscuit crumbs and nuts away from the heat until it forms a paste. With a wooden spoon, press this into the oiled tin. Flatten and smooth off the top (a cut lime or orange does this very well), mark into slices and allow to cool.

When cold, turn out on to foil, wrap and refrigerate until required. The cake keeps for some weeks.

Note

Golden syrup may be used instead of honey and a few drops of vanilla can be added to the chocolate mixture. Chopped candied peel is an alternative to the nuts.

MARTINIQUE RICE CAKE

Preparation time 10 – 12 minutes
Cooking time about 1 hour 20 minutes
Oven temperature 375°F., Gas Mark 5

You will need

1½ pints (U.S. 3¾ cups) hot milk
½ teaspoon vanilla essence
8 oz. rice
4 oz. butter
4 eggs, separated
1½ oz. castor sugar
1 tablespoon ground almonds

FOR THE TOPPING
guava jelly (see page 113)
whipped cream (optional)

Blend the milk and vanilla, add the rice and cook for about 20 minutes until rice is tender. Beat the butter to a cream, very slowly add the egg yolks beating all the time and continue beating for 5 minutes. Beat in sugar and almonds, then add the cooked rice, draining off any unabsorbed milk. Beat the egg whites very stiffly and fold them into the mixture. Pour into a buttered cake tin, put this in a tin of hot water and bake in a moderately hot oven for 1 hour.

FOR THE TOPPING
Turn out, cool and top with guava jelly and if liked, unsweetened whipped cream. The cake is very good with any sweet jam or plain as an accompaniment for stewed fruit or fruit fool.

Martinique rice cake

SUNDAY BEST COCONUT CAKE

This is a favourite Sunday delicacy in the islands where every little girl is dressed stiffly in white, like the cake, or pastel organdy, with a matching streamered hat.

Preparation time 15 – 20 minutes
Cooking time 45 minutes
Oven temperature 300°F., Gas Mark 2

You will need

4 oz. butter
8 oz. castor sugar
4 eggs, separated
4 oz. plain flour and 1 teaspoon baking powder
   or 4 oz. self-raising flour
pinch salt
2 tablespoons milk
6 oz. peeled ripe coconut, grated
½ teaspoon strained lime juice

Cream the butter with half the sugar. Beat the egg yolks and add to the mixture, beating all the time. Sift the flour with the baking powder, if used, and salt and add slowly to the butter mixture alternately with the milk. When well mixed, turn into a 9-inch square cake tin, lined with buttered paper. Beat the egg whites very stiffly and fold in the remaining sugar with the coconut and lime juice. Spread over the top of the cake mixture taking the topping right to the edges. Bake in a slow oven for 45 minutes. The cake can be served whole or cut into squares.

GARDEN CITY RICE BUNS

The 'Garden City' of the Caribbean is Georgetown in Guyana, built by the Dutch with wide, tree shaded canals, some of which are now filled in. It was in Brickdam, at the Y.W.C.A. that I first wrote down this recipe, overlooking green lawns and the pleasant white wood houses of this beautiful city.

Preparation time 8 minutes
Cooking time 40 – 45 minutes
Oven temperature 375°F., Gas Mark 5
To make about 20 buns

You will need

4 oz. rice
salt
4 oz. castor sugar
1 oz. butter
2 eggs, well beaten
8 oz. plain flour
grated rind 2 limes
about scant ½ pint (U.S. 1 cup) milk

Cook rice in boiling salted water for about 20 minutes until tender, drain. Cream the sugar and butter together, slowly add the eggs and flour alternately. Mix thoroughly before adding grated lime rind and rice with enough milk to make a batter. Almost fill greased patty tins with the mixture and bake in a moderately hot oven for 20 – 25 minutes until the buns are golden brown. Cool and serve split with butter.

JOURNEY CAKES

This is a favourite Jamaican tea-time speciality, something like a scone.

Preparation time 7 minutes
Cooking time 20 minutes
Oven temperature 425°F., Gas Mark 7
To make about 18 – 20 cakes

You will need

1 lb. plain flour and 1½ teaspoons baking
   powder or 1 lb. self-raising flour
¼ teaspoon salt
1½ oz. butter or margarine
1½ oz. lard
¼ pint (U.S. ⅔ cup) coconut milk or water

Sift the flour with the baking powder, if used and salt. Make a well in the sifted dry ingredients and rub in the fats. Slowly add the coconut milk or water to make a smooth dough. Shape into small balls and flatten the tops with a fork. Place on a greased baking sheet and bake in a hot oven for 20 minutes. Serve hot, sliced and buttered.
Note
Journey cakes or, as they are often called Johnny cakes, can be fried in hot fat instead of baking.

COLUMBUS COOKIES

Preparation time 10 minutes, plus 1 hour chilling
Cooking time 10 – 15 minutes
Oven temperature 375°F., Gas Mark 5
To make 25 cookies

You will need

6 oz. butter
8 oz. castor sugar
12 oz. plain or self-raising flour
1 egg, well beaten
2 tablespoons strong black coffee
1 tablespoon rum
2 teaspoons baking powder (if using plain flour)
$\frac{1}{2}$ teaspoon salt
3 oz. blanched nuts, cashews, almonds or peanuts, chopped

Cream the butter and sugar. Add 3 tablespoons flour to the egg, then beat in the coffee and rum. Add this to the butter and sugar mixture and continue beating until it is a soft batter. Sift the remaining flour with the baking powder, if used, and salt and add very slowly to the batter. Stir in the chopped nuts adding a little extra flour if the dough is not stiff enough to roll out. Refrigerate for 1 hour, then flour a board and roll out to $\frac{1}{4}$-inch thickness and cut into desired shapes. Bake on an ungreased baking sheet in a moderately hot oven for 10 – 15 minutes until cookies are firm and pale beige.

BANANA OATMEAL COOKIES

Preparation time 15 minutes
Cooking time about 15 minutes
Oven temperature 400°F., Gas Mark 6
To make about 40 cookies

You will need

6 oz. plain flour
$\frac{1}{2}$ teaspoon bicarbonate of soda
1 teaspoon salt
$\frac{1}{4}$ teaspoon grated nutmeg
$\frac{3}{4}$ teaspoon powdered cinnamon
6 oz. butter
7 oz. castor sugar
1 egg, beaten
2 – 3 bananas, peeled and mashed
10 oz. rolled oats
2 oz. chopped blanched peanuts or almonds

Sift together flour, soda, salt, and spices. Beat butter until creamy. Add sugar gradually and continue beating until light and fluffy. Beat in egg. Add bananas, rolled oats and nuts and mix thoroughly. Add flour mixture and blend. Drop teaspoonsful on to ungreased baking sheets, about $1\frac{1}{2}$-inches apart. Bake in a moderately hot oven for about 15 minutes or until golden brown. Cool on a rack.

Banana oatmeal cookies

BANANA BREAD

(Illustrated in colour on page 105)

This typical Caribbean tea-time speciality is quickly and easily made almost anywhere in the world.

Preparation time 10 minutes
Cooking time 30 minutes
Oven temperature 375°F., Gas Mark 5

You will need

4 oz. castor sugar
3 oz. butter
1 egg, well beaten
2 large ripe bananas, peeled and mashed
8 oz. plain flour and $\frac{1}{4}$ teaspoon baking powder or bicarbonate of soda or 8 oz. self-raising flour
pinch salt

Cream the sugar and butter, add egg and beat well. Beat in bananas. Sift the flour with baking powder or bicarbonate of soda, if used, and salt and fold into mixture. Turn into a buttered 9-inch loaf tin, and bake in a moderately hot oven for 30 minutes until golden brown.
Note
Chopped nuts and/or raisins may be added if liked.

ORANGE LOAF

(Illustrated in colour on page 105)

This is a very quickly made tea-time bread which I first tasted in Jamaica.

Preparation time 10 minutes
Cooking time 25 minutes
Oven temperature 425°F., Gas Mark 7

You will need

8 oz. plain flour and $\frac{1}{4}$ teaspoon baking powder or 8 oz. self-raising flour
pinch salt
4 oz. castor sugar
grated rind 1 orange
1 egg, well beaten
scant $\frac{1}{2}$ pint (U.S. 1 cup) strained orange juice
2 oz. cooking fat, melted
2 tablespoons coarse marmalade

Sift the flour with the baking powder, if used, salt and sugar. Add the orange rind and mix well. Blend the egg, orange juice and fat, beat a little, then stir into the flour mixture. Put the mixture into a well buttered round cake tin and spoon the marmalade on top. Bake in a hot oven for 25 minutes. Allow to cool for 5 minutes, then turn out.
Note
Extra marmalade can be spread over the top of the cake after baking if liked.

CASSAVA PONE

Preparation time 10 – 12 minutes
Cooking time $1\frac{1}{4}$ hours
Oven temperature 375°F., Gas Mark 5

You will need

2 sweet cassavas, peeled and grated
about 6 oz. peeled ripe coconut, grated
1 oz. butter
6 oz. sugar
1 teaspoon baking powder
1 teaspoon powdered allspice
1 teaspoon powdered cinnamon
1 teaspoon vanilla essence
generous $\frac{1}{4}$ pint (U.S. $\frac{3}{4}$ cup) milk
generous $\frac{1}{4}$ pint (U.S. $\frac{3}{4}$ cup) water

Mix the cassava and coconut, cut in the butter and add the sugar, baking powder, allspice, cinnamon and vanilla. Add enough liquid to bind. Grease a baking tin and put in the mixture which should come about 2 inches up the sides. Bake in a moderately hot oven for about $1\frac{1}{2}$ hours until the pone is crisp and brown. Turn out, cut into squares and serve hot or cold.
Note
The cassava can be cooked and mashed before using for a smoother pone, or dry cassava flour can be used with extra liquid. Sometimes chopped candied peel is added.
Cassava bread is quite different from the pone, it is grated cassava mixed to a dough with butter and a pinch of salt. Flat cakes are put on a baking sheet or griddle over a low heat and when steam rises, they are batted down with a wooden palette and dried in the sun. They are quite hard and dry when ready for use and are usually toasted and buttered.

Banana bread and orange loaf

Jamaican gingerbread

Guava cheese

Dutch island doughnuts

DUTCH ISLAND DOUGHNUTS

(Illustrated in colour on page 108)

Just as the waterfront buildings in Curaçao have pointed façades and roof tops, and are painted in pastel colours very reminiscent of Holland, so the food one eats is Dutch.

Preparation time 12 – 15 minutes
Cooking time 3 – 4 minutes
To make about 20 doughnuts

You will need

12 oz. plain flour and 3 teaspoons baking powder or 12 oz. self-raising flour
pinch salt
$\frac{1}{2}$ teaspoon powdered cinnamon
$\frac{1}{4}$ teaspoon grated nutmeg
12 oz. dark brown sugar
2 whole eggs, beaten
1 egg yolk
2 oz. butter, melted
generous $\frac{1}{4}$ pint (U.S. $\frac{3}{4}$ cup) milk
deep fat or oil for frying
icing sugar for dusting

Sift flour with baking powder, if used, salt, cinnamon and nutmeg and mix in sugar. Add the eggs slowly, beating lightly, then the melted butter and enough milk to make a pliable dough which is easy to handle. Flour a board and roll out the dough to a thin oblong. Cut into $1\frac{1}{2}$-2-inch wide strips and cut each strip into $3\frac{1}{2}$-inch sections. Make a slit 1-inch from one end of each strip and pull the opposite end through. Fry quickly in hot fat or oil until golden brown. Drain on absorbent paper, dust with icing sugar and serve hot or cold with guava cheese or jelly (see page 113).

JAMAICAN GINGERBREAD

(Illustrated in colour on page 106)

Preparation time 10 – 12 minutes
Cooking time $1\frac{3}{4}$ hours
Oven temperature 300°F., Gas Mark 2

You will need

2 teaspoons powdered ginger
12 oz. plain flour
2 oz. chopped mixed candied peel
2 oz. dark brown sugar
4 oz. butter
8 oz. molasses
$\frac{1}{2}$ teaspoon bicarbonate of soda
4 tablespoons warm milk
2 eggs, well beaten

TO DECORATE
candied citrus peel

Sift the ginger with the flour, add the peel and mix. Heat sugar, butter and molasses over a low heat until the sugar dissolves. Dissolve the bicarbonate of soda in the milk, add the beaten eggs and beat a little more. Add molasses mixture and egg mixture to the flour, mixing thoroughly. Line a square cake tin with buttered paper, pour in the mixture and bake at once in a slow oven for $1\frac{3}{4}$ hours. Turn out and cool. Decorate the top of the cake with thin slices of twisted citrus peel.

PICKLES, PRESERVES AND CANDIES

When fruit ripens, it is attacked by birds or falls within hours, and must be picked immediately; preserving is therefore very important. Mangoes are so profuse in some islands that the best Julies lie unwanted by the roadside. I have picked them up, sweet and delicious, in suburban Kingston, and all across the mountains in Puerto Rico, small boys offer them from full baskets for a few cents. There is a saying in Jamaica, 'Mango time, pot bottom turn up', meaning turn the pot upside down on the stove, stop cooking, there are mangoes for everyone! Jam and chutney are easy to make, bringing the indefinably delicate flavour of mangoes to the table long after the last fruit is eaten.

Sugar and spice . . . these are the backdrop to many of the islands. Children find natural candy in cane which they chew going home from school; once 'crop' begins and the fat stalks lie around to be picked up, there is a trail of chewed cane along every path through the fields. Perhaps it is the heat, but the energy produced by sugar seems essential and there are many old Caribbean family recipes for candy. I do not propose to take up valuable space with fudge, which most cooks know how to make, but try it with brown sugar, flavoured with rum and rum soaked raisins.

Citrus is available for marmalade and some unusual fruits for jam. Guava cheese, which is not cheese, but a very thick, sweet conserve is frequently made.

Preserves should be packed observing the rules; use *hot* sterile jars leaving half to one inch free at the top, depending on the size of the jar. Seal by any of the patent methods or two layers of melted candle wax covered with cellophane or greaseproof paper and held tightly by a rubber band makes as good a cap as any. A pressure cooker is excellent for sterilising jars, small bottles, caps and corks. Early morning is the time for preserving in the islands; blessed by breezes, almost every morning and evening is suitable for bulk cooking.

PEPPER SAUCE

Preparation time 5 minutes
Cooking time 20 minutes
To yield about $\frac{3}{4}$ pint (U.S. 2 cups)

You will need

8 chillis, de-seeded and chopped
1 medium-sized onion, chopped
1 teaspoon salt
3 teaspoons dry mustard
$\frac{1}{2}$ pint (U.S. $1\frac{1}{4}$ cups) vinegar
1 tablespoon olive oil

Put all the ingredients into a saucepan and mix well. Bring to the boil and simmer for 20 minutes. Fill a hot sterilised bottle with the sauce, using a funnel. Seal and store. Use as required.

Note
A little minced garlic may be added and some housewives add a chopped green pawpaw to the mixture.

MANGO CHUTNEY

In Jamaica, we made this chutney to use the surplus of lower grade fruit.

Preparation time 15 – 20 minutes
Cooking time about 45 minutes
To yield about 6 lb.

You will need

8 green mangoes
brown sugar
2 pints (U.S. 5 cups) cane or malt vinegar
2 chillis, de-seeded and chopped
1 onion, chopped
1 clove garlic, minced
4 oz. peeled green ginger, chopped
1 teaspoon whole allspice
4 oz. seedless raisins, soaked in rum for 15
　　minutes, if liked

Peel mangoes, remove stones and cut up. Just cover the fruit with water and simmer until tender, about 15 minutes. Drain and weigh the fruit. Stir the same weight of sugar into 1½ pints (U.S. 3¾ cups) vinegar, bring to the boil and cook until syrupy. Moisten the chillis, onion, garlic, and ginger with the remaining vinegar, add to the syrup with the cooked mangoes, allspice and raisins. Boil gently until the mixture thickens, about 15 – 20 minutes. Cool, pour into hot sterile jars, seal and store.

CHOW CHOW

Preparation time 15 minutes, plus overnight
　　　　　　　　soaking
Cooking time about 15 minutes
To yield about 6 lb.

You will need

3 cucumbers, peeled and chopped
8 small onions, thinly sliced
3 green tomatoes, quartered
12 string beans, tips and strings removed
1 cauliflower, broken up into flowerets
2 chillis, de-seeded and chopped
2 pints (U.S. 5 cups) water
6 tablespoons salt
2 pints (U.S. 5 cups) wine vinegar
2 oz. flour
8 oz. granulated sugar
1 teaspoon turmeric
3 tablespoons dry mustard

Wash all the vegetables and stand in the water with the salt overnight. Next day, drain, rinse the vegetables in clear water, put in a saucepan with the vinegar and very slowly bring to the boil. Take a little of the hot vinegar to mix the flour, sugar, turmeric and mustard to a smooth paste. Stir this into the boiling vegetable mixture and cook for 5 minutes, stirring all the time. Fill hot, sterile jars, seal and store.

Mango chutney

Chow chow

SPICED PICKLED LIMES

Preparation time 5 minutes
Cooking time 7½ minutes
To yield about 1½ lb.

You will need

12 firm limes, cut in ¼-inch slices
1¼ lb. granulated or light brown sugar
pinch salt
½ pint (U.S. 1¼ cups) cane or malt vinegar
3 tablespoons water
2-inch stick cinnamon
1 teaspoon whole allspice
2 oz. peeled green ginger, chopped
4 cloves

Remove pips from lime slices. Mix the sugar, salt and vinegar with the water. Tie the spices in muslin and add, then boil the mixture for 5 minutes. Add the lime slices and continue cooking for a further 2½ minutes. Discard the spices, pack the lime slices into hot sterile jars and fill up with hot syrup. Seal and store.

OLD SOUR

Preparation time 5 minutes
To yield 1 pint (U.S. 2½ cups)

You will need

1 pint (U.S. 2½ cups) strained lime juice
1 tablespoon salt
pinch cayenne pepper (optional)

Pour the lime juice into a hot sterilised bottle, add the salt and shake until dissolved. Add the cayenne if a hotter condiment is liked. The old sour will keep almost indefinitely but must be stored for a fortnight before use to allow for fermentation. Use as a hot sauce for sprinkling on fish or meat.

BIRD PEPPER SAUCE

Bird peppers are very hot, small red peppers.

Preparation time 5 minutes
To yield ½ pint (U.S. 1¼ cups)

You will need

8 bird peppers
about ½ pint (U.S. 1¼ cups) cooking sherry

Half fill a stoppered bottle with the bird peppers. Pour over sherry and as the sherry is used, top up again once or twice. Use in soups and stews.

MANGO JAM

Preparation time about 10 minutes
Cooking time about 45 minutes

You will need

slightly under-ripe mangoes
granulated sugar

Peel mangoes, remove stones and cut up. Put mango flesh in a pan, just cover with water, bring to the boil and cook until soft, about 15 – 20 minutes. Turn into a sieve, allow juice to strain through into a bowl, then rub the pulp through, discarding the remaining strings. Measure the mango pulp. Put it back into pan with an equal quantity of sugar. Bring to boil and simmer until the mixture forms a jelly when dropped on to a cold plate. Pour into hot sterile jars, seal and store.

GUAVA CHEESE

(Illustrated in colour on page 107)

Preparation time about 5 minutes
Cooking time about 35 – 45 minutes

You will need

guavas
granulated sugar
icing sugar

Cut tops off guavas and rub through a sieve. Weigh pulp and put in a saucepan with the same weight of granulated sugar. Bring to the boil and simmer over a medium heat until mixture becomes stiff and shrinks from the sides of the pan. Turn out into a greased and sugared tin. When cold dredge with icing sugar and cut into squares. Make certain that the cheese is thoroughly dry before storing in a tin.

GUAVA JELLY

Preparation time about 5 minutes
Cooking time about 45 – 50 minutes

You will need

guavas
granulated sugar
strained lime juice

Cut the tops off the guavas, put in a saucepan and just cover with water. Cook over a medium heat until soft, about 15 – 20 minutes. Strain off the resulting juice, measure it, and put it back in the saucepan with an equal quantity of sugar. Add ½ teaspoon lime juice to each ½ pint (U.S. 1¼ cups) liquid. Reheat the mixture, stirring until the sugar dissolves. Bring to the boil, skim and continue boiling until the mixture forms a jelly when dropped on to a cold plate. Pour into hot sterile jars, seal and store.

Note
The pulp remaining after the guava juice has been strained is sometimes used for guava cheese; it is satisfactory, but the flavour is not as sharp as that made from the previous recipe. I have used the pulp, mixed with plain ice cream to make a pleasant dessert.

MARJORAM LIME JELLY

Preparation time 5 minutes, plus 30 minutes steeping
Cooking time about 10 minutes
To yield 2 lb.

You will need

½ pint (U.S. 1¼ cups) boiling water
2 tablespoons chopped marjoram
6 tablespoons strained lime juice
1½ lb. granulated sugar
5 tablespoons pectin or 1½ oz. gelatine dissolved in 4 tablespoons hot water

Pour boiling water on to marjoram and set aside for 30 minutes. Strain the liquid into a saucepan. Add lime juice and sugar and stir until dissolved. Bring to the boil, add the pectin or gelatine, bring to the boil once more and boil for ½ minute. Remove from heat, cool, skim the top and pour into hot sterile jars. Seal and store.

MIXED FRUIT MARMALADE

Preparation time 20 minutes, plus overnight soaking
Cooking time about 2 hours
To yield about 8 lb.

You will need

1 grapefruit
1 orange
2 limes or 1 lemon
1 small pineapple or can of pineapple
2½ pints (U.S. 6¼ cups) water
5 lb. granulated sugar

Thinly peel the citrus rind and shred. Peel away pith, chop the fruit and put the pips in a muslin bag. Peel pineapple, discard the peel and chop. Put the fruit, citrus peel and pips to soak in the water and set aside for at least 12 hours. When soaked, put in a saucepan with the water in which the fruit soaked, bring to the boil and simmer for about 1½ hours, until the peel is tender. Discard the bag of pips, stir in the sugar and boil until the mixture sets when dropped on to a plate. Pour into hot sterile jars, seal and store.

Note
The marmalade can be made without the pineapple and using 1 lb. less sugar.

Mixed fruit marmalade

SPICED WATERMELON

(Illustrated in colour on page 117)

Preparation time 7 – 10 minutes
Cooking time   about 40 minutes
To yield   about 2 lb.

You will need

1 watermelon
1½ pints (U.S. 3¾ cups) water
4 pieces ginger
2-inch stick cinnamon
1 teaspoon whole allspice
4 cloves
sugar

Halve and quarter the melon, remove most of the red flesh and use for another purpose. Peel the rind off very thinly and cut the pale green flesh into ¾-inch pieces. Put the melon in a saucepan with the water and ginger, tie the spices in a muslin bag and add. Bring to the boil and simmer until the melon is tender, about 20 minutes. Drain the juice and measure it, adding an equal quantity of sugar. Stir until the sugar dissolves, add the fruit, ginger and spices, bring to the boil and simmer for a further 15 minutes. Discard spices and pack melon into hot sterilised jars, filling up with boiling syrup. Seal and store.

JAMAICAN FRUITS IN RUM

Preparation time 10 minutes, plus 1 hour
                standing
To yield   about 8 lb.

You will need

2 tangerines
3 mangoes
1 lb. strawberries, hulled
½ pineapple, peeled and diced
2-inch stick cinnamon
2 lb. brown sugar
2 lb. granulated sugar
1½ pints (U.S. 3¾ cups) rum

Peel tangerines, including all the pith, divide into segments and discard pips. Peel mangoes, remove stones and slice. Put the fruits in a large bowl with the cinnamon stick. Add the sugars and toss the fruit. Set aside for 1 hour turning the fruit over three or four times to ensure even distribution of sugar. Pack into a large sterile jar and cover with rum. Seal and do not open for 3 months.
Note
Any garden fruit can be used in this manner, the rum, when strained off, makes a pleasant liqueur drink.

PRESERVED PINEAPPLE FRUIT MELANGE

Preparation time about 20 minutes
Cooking time   40 minutes

You will need

FOR THE BASIC PINEAPPLE PRESERVE
2 medium-sized pineapples
1 pint (U.S. 2½ cups) water
3 lb. sugar
1 tablespoon powdered allspice
1 tablespoon coriander seeds
1½-inch stick cinnamon
1 sprig thyme
1 pint (U.S. 2½ cups) rum

FOR THE FRUIT MELANGE
Any fruits in season, such as bananas, mangoes, melon, garden cherries and strawberries (excluding citrus)
weight of added fruit in sugar

FOR THE BASIC PINEAPPLE PRESERVE
Peel pineapples and cut into ¾-inch cubes. Put half the pineapple cubes into a saucepan with the water and simmer over a medium heat for 35 minutes. Remove from heat, strain off the juice and add 8 oz. sugar. Add the spices tied in a muslin bag and return to the heat for a further 5 minutes. Pour into a large wide necked jar, add the rum, pineapple and sugar. Stir until the sugar dissolves.

FOR THE FRUIT MELANGE
Allow to cool, then add any desired fruits such as thinly sliced bananas, cubes of melon, thinly sliced mangoes, halved and stoned garden cherries and hulled strawberries. (Citrus fruits are unsuitable as the acid tends to make the mélange ferment). Add the weight of the fruit in sugar. Seal and store in a cool place. This preserved fruit mélange is delicious with any plain dessert, ice cream, rice or custard.

PRESERVED PINEAPPLE

Preparation time   about 8 minutes, plus 24 hours standing
Cooking time $1\frac{1}{2}$ – $1\frac{3}{4}$ hours
To yield   about 3 – 4 lb.

You will need

1 large or 2 small pineapples
$1\frac{1}{4}$ lb. granulated sugar
$1\frac{1}{2}$ pints (U.S. $3\frac{3}{4}$ cups) water

Peel pineapple and cut into 1-inch cubes. Put into a saucepan with half the sugar and the water, bring to the boil and cook over a moderate heat for 1 hour. Cover and set aside overnight. Next day, drain the syrup into another saucepan, add the remaining sugar and bring to the boil. Add the fruit and simmer until the syrup is thick and the fruit transparent. Cover and set aside once again overnight. Next day, drain the syrup and pack the fruit into hot sterile jars. Boil up the syrup and cook until it becomes very thick, almost a jelly, then spoon it over the fruit in the jars. Seal and store.

CANDIED CITRUS PEEL

Preparation time   10 minutes
Cooking time   about 45 minutes
To yield   about 2 lb.

You will need

4 small oranges, 2 grapefruit, 4 lemons or 5 limes
$1\frac{1}{2}$ pints (U.S. $3\frac{3}{4}$ cups) water
8 oz. granulated sugar

Peel the chosen fruit in long strips. Put the strips in a saucepan covered with the water, bring slowly to the boil and boil until tender. Drain, scrape the pith off the inside of the peel with a sharp knife and cut peel into wedges. Make a syrup with the sugar and 2 tablespoons water. Boil the peel in the syrup until nearly all is absorbed and the peel is semi-transparent. Dry in the hot sun or in a warm oven. Store in a dry, air-tight jar.
Note
Some people add 2 tablespoons molasses to the sugar syrup and roll the transparent peel in granulated sugar. A delicious alternative is to roll it in melted dark chocolate and dry it on greaseproof paper.

SPICED NUTS

Preparation time   7 minutes
Cooking time $2\frac{1}{2}$ hours
Oven temperature   275°F., Gas Mark 1
To make   2 lb.

You will need

1 lb. castor sugar
2 teaspoons salt
$\frac{1}{4}$ teaspoon grated nutmeg
3 teaspoons powdered cinnamon
2 teaspoons powdered ginger
2 teaspoons powdered allspice
2 egg whites, beaten with 2 tablespoons water
1 lb. blanched mixed nuts, such as cashews, pecans and almonds.

Sift the sugar with the salt and all the spices. Put the beaten egg white mixture in a bowl and put the nuts in a wire sieve that will fit into the bowl. Dip the nuts in egg white and shake well to coat and drain. Put most of the sugar in a large jar, add the nuts a few at a time and shake well to coat with sugar. Shake some of the spiced sugar on to a baking sheet, lay the nuts on top, sprinkle again with sugar and bake in a very slow oven for $2\frac{1}{2}$ hours. Cool, then shake the nuts once again in the spiced sugar and store in a tightly closed jar.

Spiced nuts

VANILLA ANGELS

Preparation time 5 – 8 minutes
Cooking time about 5 minutes
To make about 1½ lb.

You will need

8 oz. corn syrup
12 oz. castor sugar
6 tablespoons water
pinch salt
2 egg whites
1 teaspoon vanilla essence
about 24 blanched nuts, coarsely chopped or
    2 oz. unsweetened chocolate, grated

Heat corn syrup with the sugar, water and salt until the syrup forms a hard ball when dropped into a bowl of cold water. Stiffly whisk egg whites and add syrup, beating for 2 minutes with a rotary beater and continuing for a further 2 minutes with a wooden spoon. Add vanilla and continue beating until mixture thickens and forms peaks when dropped from the spoon. Quickly stir in nuts, if used, and drop by the spoonful on to oiled paper. Alternatively, pour mixture into an oiled 8-inch tin, sprinkled with grated bitter chocolate. Cut into squares when set.

PINEAPPLE DELIGHT

Preparation time 10 minutes
Cooking time about 10 minutes
To make about 1½ lb.

You will need

1 large pineapple
1 lb. granulated sugar

Peel and grate pineapple. Heat the sugar over a low heat, stir in the grated pineapple and continue cooking until the mixture forms a thread when dropped from a spoon into a bowl of cold water. Remove from the heat and beat with a rotary beater for 3 minutes. Pour into an oiled 8-inch cake tin and allow to cool and set. Cut into squares.

BITTER SWEET CHEWS

Preparation time 7 minutes
Cooking time 5 minutes
To make about 1½ lb.

You will need

8 oz. butter or margarine
12 oz. granulated sugar
about 24 blanched cashew nuts, coarsely
    chopped
2 teaspoons Angostura Bitters
8 oz. plain chocolate, grated

Melt the butter and sugar and cook over a low heat, stirring until well mixed. Continue cooking for a further 2 minutes, stirring all the time. Remove from the heat, stir in nuts and Angostura and pour into an oiled 8-inch tin. Sprinkle thickly with grated chocolate, spreading the chips evenly over the surface. Set aside to cool, marking into squares when half set. Break up when hard.

TULOONS

Preparation time 5 minutes
Cooking time about 5 minutes
To make about 2 lb.

You will need

1 lb. molasses
2 oz. brown sugar
2 tablespoons powdered ginger
9 oz. peeled ripe coconut, grated
about 12 blanched peanuts, halved

Heat the molasses with the sugar and ginger until the syrup forms a thread when dropped from a spoon into a bowl of cold water. Remove from the heat, add the coconut and beat until the mixture thickens enough to form balls when dropped from the spoon. Drop by the spoonful on to oiled paper and allow to cool. When cool, but not set, press a half nut on to each spoonful.

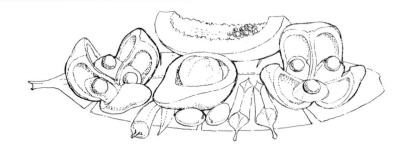

Spiced watermelon

Luncheon bowl

DRINKS

'The chief fudling they make on the island is Rumbullion, alias Kill-Devil, and this is made of sugar canes distilled, a hot, hellish and terrible liquor', writes a traveller of Barbados in the 17th century. 'Kill-Devil' (or rum) became, and remained, the established drink of the islands, 'very requisite where so much heat is, for the spirits being exhausted with much sweating, the inner parts are left cold and faint and shall need comforting'. Sailors, combating gales round the islands, spoke of the 'comfort waters' and there are prim, uninspiring references in old books to 'Barbados waters'.

Sugar is so interwoven with West Indian history, that rum has become the very essence of the Carib-bean. The name may derive from the Spanish *ron*, or it could be from the Greek *sakcharon* or Latin *saccharum*. Some say it stems from Devonshire dialect, *rumbooze* or *rumbustion* or from the 18th century *rumbo*. Rum has now emerged from the shadowy image of drunken seamen and modern connoisseurs, not content to drink from the cask like their forefathers, demand such refinements as Rum Frappé or Bishop's Punch with brandy. All rums leave the still colourless, acquiring slight colour from the cask while ageing. Different shades come from caramel, and very dark rum simply has more added colouring. The paler the better is today's rum fashion.

FALERNUM

Preparation time 5 minutes
Heating time 5 minutes
To make 5 – 6 pints (U.S. 12½ – 15) cups

You will need

2 lb. granulated sugar
5 pints (U.S. 12½ cups) water
¼ pint (U.S. ⅔ cup) strained lime juice
6 drops almond essence
1 pint (U.S. 2½ cups) white rum (optional)

Heat sugar and half the water in a saucepan until sugar has dissolved. Cool, add lime juice, almond essence, remaining water and rum, if liked. Serve by itself or mixed with other drinks as a sweetener.

BASIC SUGAR SYRUP

Preparation time 2 minutes
Cooking time about 10 minutes
To make about ¾ pint (U.S. 2 cups)

You will need

¼ pint (U.S. ⅔ cup) water
1 lb. sugar

Put water and sugar into a saucepan over a medium heat until sugar has dissolved. Boil for about 10 minutes, then bottle.

LUNCHEON BOWL

(Illustrated in colour on page 118)

Preparation time 5 minutes, plus standing and chilling time
To make about 24 glasses

You will need

6 sprigs marjoram, bruised
2 tablespoons castor sugar
scant ½ pint (U.S. 1 cup) rum
1 bottle still white wine
2 bottles sparkling red wine
1 pint (U.S. 2½ cups) soda water
3 limes, thinly sliced
cracked ice

Put the marjoram in a bowl covered with the sugar. Pour the rum over and allow to stand for 30 minutes. Add the still wine and chill. At the same time chill the sparkling wine and soda water and pour these into the bowl just before serving. Remove marjoram and float slices of lime on top. A quarter fill cups or glasses with cracked ice and fill from the bowl.

TRINIDAD HILTON RUM PUNCH

Preparation time 5 minutes
To make about 12 glasses

You will need

½ pint (U.S. 1¼ cups) strained lime juice
¼ pint (U.S. ⅔ cup) strained orange juice
¼ pint (U.S. ⅔ cup) strained pineapple juice
2 tablespoons basic sugar syrup (see page 119)
2 – 3 dashes Angostura Bitters
¾ pint (U.S. 2 cups) rum
cracked ice
grated nutmeg
halved pineapple slices
orange slices
cherries

Mix all the ingredients except the ice and fruit in a bowl. Half-fill cups with cracked ice, fill up with punch, sprinkle with nutmeg and float pineapple and orange slices, and cherries on top.

BLUE MOUNTAIN PUNCH

This is the punch to drink on the high peaks in the cool early morning.

Preparation time 5 minutes
Heating time 5 minutes
To make about 12 glasses

You will need

1 tablespoon powdered ginger
1 teaspoon grated nutmeg
3 pints (U.S. 7½ cups) warmed beer
3 eggs
2 tablespoons molasses
scant ¼ pint (U.S. ½ cup) rum

Blend the ginger and nutmeg with 2½ pints (U.S. 6¾ cups) beer and heat. Beat the eggs with the remaining beer and molasses. Add the warm beer to the egg mixture a little at a time, beating all the time. Add the rum and serve at once.

SHIRLEY'S WEST INDIA COMMITTEE PUNCH

This recipe comes from Mrs. Shirley Hobson of the West India Committee in London. The Committee will supply information on any Caribbean territory.

Preparation time 5 minutes
To make about 6 glasses

You will need

¼ pint (U.S. ⅔ cup) strained grapefruit juice
¼ pint (U.S. ⅔ cup) strained lime juice
2 tablespoons maraschino
1 tablespoon golden syrup
2 dashes Angostura Bitters
1 pint (U.S. 2½ cups) rum
cracked ice or small ice cubes
6 slices fresh lime or lemon
6 maraschino cherries

Shake all the ingredients, except the ice, lime or lemon and cherries. Half-fill cups or glasses with cracked ice, pour on the punch and top with a lime or lemon slice and a cherry.

BISHOP'S PUNCH

Preparation time 5 minutes
To make   about 12 glasses

You will need

4 tablespoons brandy
scant ¼ pint (U.S. ½ cup) rum
scant ¼ pint (U.S. ½ cup) peach brandy
½ pint (U.S. 1¼ cups) strained lime juice
12 oz. castor sugar
2½ pints (U.S. 6¼ cups) soda water
6 – 8 ice cubes

Mix brandy, rum, peach brandy and lime juice and pour on to sugar in a large bowl. When sugar has dissolved, add soda water and ice. Serve in punch cups.

GREAT HOUSE JAMAICAN RUM PUNCH

Preparation time 5 minutes
To make   about 12 glasses

You will need

1 pint (U.S. 2½ cups) rum
4½ tablespoons strained lime juice
4½ tablespoons strained orange juice
3 tablespoons honey
cracked ice
4 tablespoons water
grated nutmeg

Mix, with a rotary beater in the punch bowl, all the ingredients except ice, water and nutmeg. Fill each punch cup half-full with cracked ice and fill up with punch. Add a teaspoon of water to each cup and a pinch of grated nutmeg. Stir before serving.

RUM COLLINS

Preparation time 2 minutes
To make   1 glass

Rum collins

You will need

2 tablespoons strained lime juice
1 teaspoon sugar
3 tablespoons rum
3 – 4 ice cubes
soda water
2 slices lime
1 maraschino cherry

Mix the lime juice with the sugar until dissolved. Add the rum, pour on to the ice cubes in a frosted glass, top up with soda water and decorate with lime slices and a cherry, on a cocktail stick.

RUM MINT JULEP

Preparation time 5 minutes
To make   1 glass

You will need

3 sprigs mint
1 teaspoon sugar
1 tablespoon water
cracked ice
3 tablespoons rum

Place 2 mint sprigs in the bottom of a tall glass, sprinkle with sugar, add the water and pound until the sugar dissolves and the mint is well bruised. Remove mint, fill the glass three-quarters full with cracked ice, pour in the rum and top with the remaining sprig of mint.

RUM SANTA

Preparation time 5 minutes, plus chilling time
To make   1 glass

You will need

1 Seville orange
2 tablespoons molasses
5 tablespoons cold water
3 tablespoons rum
cracked ice

Peel a piece of the orange for decoration and squeeze juice. Mix the orange juice, molasses and water, stir until dissolved. Strain and chill in a tall glass, then add the rum and leave for a few minutes to settle. Strain into a clean glass, half-filled with cracked ice and decorate with orange rind.

GOOD HOPE

Preparation time 3 minutes
To make   1 glass

You will need

1 egg
1 teaspoon sugar
few drops vanilla essence
cracked ice
3 tablespoons rum
about 5 tablespoons ice cold milk
grated nutmeg

Blend all the ingredients, except the milk and nutmeg, in an electric blender or with a rotary beater. Pour into a tall chilled glass, top up with cold milk and sprinkle with nutmeg.

RUM SWIZZLE

The swizzle stick originated in Guyana and it was at Lama, where canals are dammed in a U formation to feed the sugar lands, that I learnt all about swizzles.

Rum swizzle

Preparation time 2 minutes
To make   1 glass

You will need

2 teaspoons castor sugar
2 tablespoons strained lime juice
2 sprigs mint
3 tablespoons rum
cracked ice

Put everything, except ice, in a jug, reserving 1 mint sprig for decorating, and using a swizzle stick, swirl and swizzle until mixture is frothy. Pour on to cracked ice and serve at once, decorated with mint.

BANANA DAIQUIRI

Daiquiri is a St. Thomas, U.S. Virgin Islands, speciality. I found exactly the same drink served at a small restaurant in England, The Old School House at Ockley in Sussex.

Preparation time 2 minutes
To make   1 glass

You will need

1 banana, peeled and chopped
1 tablespoon strained orange juice
3 tablespoons rum
cracked ice

Mix banana and orange juice in an electric blender or with a rotary beater. Add the rum and serve in a chilled glass with cracked ice.

ANGOSTURA SCORPION

Preparation time 2 minutes
To make 1 glass

You will need

2 tablespoons basic sugar syrup (see page 119)
2 tablespoons strained lime juice
dash Angostura Bitters
3 tablespoons rum
cracked ice

Shake all the ingredients and pour into a chilled cocktail glass.

GINGER LIMEADE

Preparation time 10 minutes, plus overnight standing and chilling time
Cooking time 35 minutes
To make 6 – 8 glasses

You will need

juice 6 limes
2 tablespoons cold water
4 – 5 slices green ginger, scraped
5 cloves
1 teaspoon whole allspice
2 pints (U.S. 5 cups) boiling water
1½ lb. granulated sugar

Strain the lime juice, add the cold water and set aside overnight. Next day, handle the juice carefully so as not to disturb the sediment and strain again. Put the ginger, cloves and allspice into the boiling water and simmer for 20 minutes. Strain, add the sugar, stir, add the lime juice, bring to the boil and simmer for a further 15 minutes. Strain once more and allow to cool. Bottle and chill. This drink will keep for a few days.

SOURSOP PUNCH

Preparation time 10 minutes, plus chilling time
To make 4 glasses

You will need

1 soursop, peeled
¾ pint (U.S. 2 cups) water
6 tablespoons condensed milk
pinch salt
1½ oz. castor sugar

Crush the soursop in a bowl with half the water. Pound it well, then rub through a sieve to extract the juice. Add the remaining water, mix and sieve again. Add condensed milk and salt, and stir in the sugar until dissolved. Strain once more, chill and serve in chilled tumblers.

NURSERY PUNCH

Preparation time 5 minutes
To make 1 glass

You will need

1 banana, peeled and mashed
strained juice 1 orange
generous ¼ pint (U.S. ¾ cup) ice cold milk
2 tablespoons honey
1 tablespoon ice cream

Blend the ingredients in an electric blender or with a rotary beater. Pour quickly into a chilled tumbler. and top with ice cream.

Nursery punch

PAWPAW AND GRAPEFRUIT PUNCH

Preparation time 10 minutes, plus chilling time
To make 4 glasses

You will need

1 medium-sized pawpaw
6 tablespoons condensed milk
strained juice 2 grapefruit
2 oz. castor sugar
¾ pint (U.S. 2 cups) water

Halve the pawpaw, discard the seeds, scoop out the pulp and mash. Mix with the milk, in an electric blender or with a rotary beater. Mix grapefruit juice with sugar and water. Blend grapefruit with pawpaw mixture, whisking well. Chill and serve in tall glasses.

CHRISTMAS EGG NOG

(Illustrated in colour on page 57)

Egg nog is the traditional drink for Christmas morning on many of the islands, to be followed by a very late lunch.

Preparation time 15 minutes, plus 4 hours chilling
To make 6 glasses

You will need

6 eggs, separated
8 oz. castor sugar
½ pint (U.S. 1¼ cups) milk
scant ¼ pint (U.S. ½ cup) Cognac
scant ¼ pint (U.S. ½ cup) dark Jamaican rum
½ pint (U.S. 1¼ cups) double cream, lightly whipped
coarsely grated rind 1 orange
finely grated rind 1 lime
grated nutmeg

Beat the egg yolks with the sugar until thick and creamy. Stir in the milk, brandy and rum. Whisk the egg whites until very stiff and fold into the mixture. Chill for about 4 hours. Fold cream into the egg mixture with the orange and lime rind. Pour into glasses or cups and top with grated nutmeg.

RUM COFFEE ON THE ROCKS

Preparation time 5 minutes
To make 6 tall glasses

You will need

ice cubes
generous ¼ pint (U.S. ¾ cup) rum
1 pint (U.S. 2½ cups) triple strength cold black coffee
6 tablespoons double cream, lightly whipped
sugar (optional)

Put about 3 ice cubes in each tall glass, pour on 1½ tablespoons rum, fill up with black coffee and top with whipped cream. Add sugar if liked.
Note
Double strength coffee can be used instead of triple strength, if preferred and fresh ground or instant coffee can be used.

RUM COFFEE AND BITTER CHOCOLATE

Preparation time 5 minutes
To make 6 – 8 cups

You will need

6 oz. unsweetened chocolate
½ teaspoon powdered cinnamon
½ teaspoon vanilla essence
generous ¼ pint (U.S. ¾ cup) rum
1 pint (U.S. 2½ cups) double strength cold black coffee
6 tablespoons double cream, lightly whipped
sugar (optional)

Melt the chocolate in a basin over a pan of boiling water. Stir in the cinnamon and vanilla. When well mixed, add the rum and slowly stir in the coffee. Chill and serve in cups topped with whipped cream. Add sugar if liked.

Grenada spiced chocolate

GRENADA SPICED CHOCOLATE

They say the people in Grenada walk with a dancing step and that this comes from generations of 'dancing cocoa'. The cocoa beans are polished by people walking, or rather dancing, over them.

Preparation time 5 minutes
Cooking time 35 minutes
To make 6 cups

You will need

4 oz. bitter chocolate
$\frac{1}{4}$ pint (U.S. $\frac{2}{3}$ cup) boiling water
$1\frac{1}{2}$ pints (U.S. $3\frac{3}{4}$ cups) milk
$\frac{1}{2}$ pint (U.S. $1\frac{1}{4}$ cups) single cream
3 oz. castor sugar
pinch salt
$\frac{1}{4}$ teaspoon grated nutmeg
$\frac{1}{2}$ teaspoon powdered allspice
2 teaspoons powdered cinnamon
2 eggs
2 teaspoons vanilla essence

Melt chocolate in the top of a double saucepan or basin over boiling water. When melted, add the boiling water and stir until smooth. Stir in the milk, cream, sugar, salt, nutmeg, allspice and cinnamon. Cook in the top of the double saucepan or basin, for 30 minutes, beating at 5 minute intervals. Beat the eggs with the vanilla, add a little of the hot chocolate and beat again, then stir into the rest of the hot chocolate mixture. Remove from the heat, beat briskly and serve hot with thin dry toast.

CAFE BRULOT

Preparation time 5 minutes
Heating time 5 minutes
To make 6 – 8 demitasse

You will need

2 pieces orange rind
2 pieces lime or lemon rind
6 sugar lumps
3 cloves
2-inch stick cinnamon
$\frac{1}{2}$ teaspoon vanilla essence
$\frac{3}{4}$ pint (U.S. 2 cups) rum
$\frac{3}{4}$ pint (U.S. 2 cups) strong black coffee

Put orange and lime or lemon rind in a saucepan with 4 sugar lumps, cloves, cinnamon and vanilla. Add the rum and very slowly bring nearly to boiling point. Dip a warmed ladle into the spiced rum, fill and drop 2 sugar lumps into the ladle. Ignite and when flaming, gently lower the ladle into the saucepan of rum. Add the coffee and wait until the rum has stopped burning. Strain into small cups.

Barbecued fresh tuna steaks

126

EATING OUT OF DOORS

The feeling for outdoor cookery is increasing everywhere. Open air living is the obvious answer in a hot climate but some of its delights can be savoured on a summer's day or night in any country garden, on the deck of a boat or in a town house patio. Picnics are always a childhood thrill, lunch on the beach brings nostalgic nursery memories for some, but it takes a Caribbean holiday to demonstrate eating outside at its best. Almost every hotel produces an attractive array of cold food on the lunch buffet, the aroma of sizzling meat wafts up from an open grill on the beach and succulent sandwiches are always on the menu.

In this chapter there is only space for a few of the most original dishes which not only look attractive but are also easy to serve. Edam Fish Cheese is a Dutch Antilles recipe which I have not been offered anywhere else, the Isles of June fruit salad looks pretty anywhere, but surrounded by tropical flowers on a veranda table covered with big leaves, it appears even better.

Skewered food is excellent for eating outside, there are inumerable combinations given here and the reader can think out many more. Sandwiches are useful for unexpected guests or, served hot, for a simple lunch.

BARBECUED FRESH TUNA STEAKS

Preparation time	10 minutes, plus 3 hours marinating
Cooking time	about 16 minutes
To serve	4 – 6

You will need

FOR THE MARINADE
¼ pint (U.S. ⅔ cup) strained lime juice
¼ pint (U.S. ⅔ cup) olive oil
1 tablespoon grated horseradish (optional)
2 eschalots or spring onions, finely chopped
1 tablespoon crushed thyme
1½ teaspoons salt
¼ teaspoon pepper
2 teaspoons Worcestershire sauce
3 tablespoons rum

FOR THE FISH
4 – 6 tuna steaks, cut in 1½-inch slices

FOR THE MARINADE
Mix all the ingredients together.

FOR THE FISH
Add the fish to the marinade and leave for 3 hours before use, turning once. Drain fish, reserving marinade for basting. Grill over a medium heat for about 8 minutes on each side, basting frequently. Serve with lime wedges.

Note
Other fish steaks can be used instead of tuna, such as dolphin, kingfish and salmon.

QUAIL OR TEAL COOKED IN ASHES

Preparation time 10 minutes
Cooking time about 35 – 40 minutes
To serve 4

You will need

4 quail or teal
4 – 6 tablespoons sweet potato stuffing (see page 69)
4 breadfruit or banana leaves or other very large leaves
4 slices fat salt pork

Stuff the birds with sweet potato stuffing and sew them up. Cut the leaves to the correct size for completely wrapping the birds. Wrap each bird in a leaf, making a small parcel and secure with thread. Tie a slice of pork over each parcel and finally wrap in greased foil. Put the birds in the hot ashes of a wood fire and cook for 35 – 40 minutes. Keep the fire going so that the birds can be continually surrounded with fresh hot ash. When cooked, unwrap the foil and discard the pork. Open out the leaves and serve the birds on the leaves in which they cooked. Serve with Hunter's Orange Sauce (see page 29).
Note
Plantains may be cooked in the same ashes, the skins slit as for Barbecued Bananas (see page 133). If already half-cooked, breadfruit are delicious cooked in the ashes, wrapped in greased foil.

TREE OYSTER KEBAB

Preparation time about 10 minutes, plus thawing time
Cooking time about 20 – 30 minutes
To serve 5 or 10 (see below)

You will need

1 large frozen turkey
barbecue sauce for turkey (see page 132)
5 or 10 slices peeled pineapple (see below)

Cut across the breastbone of the turkey and remove both ends, together with the leg and wing joints; these will not be used and should be kept frozen until required. Cut the remaining breastbone into about 5 steaks. If possible ask your butcher to do this for you, or use an electric carving knife or a chopper.

Lay the steaks flat in a large pan, stacked if necessary. As they thaw, sprinkle with the barbecue sauce. When thawed out, brush with the juices and the sauce, well mixed, making sure that each steak is coated. Split each steak in two down the breastbone for average servings, or leave whole for large servings; in each case there will be a mixture of dark and light meat for each person. Grill for about 10 – 15 minutes on each side, keeping the turkey about 6 inches from the coals on a rack. Heat pineapple slices for the last 3 minutes of cooking. Serve steaks on a pineapple slice well covered with the remaining sauce.

VEAL CHEESE KEBABS

Preparation time 5 minutes, plus 2 hours marinating
Cooking time about 20 minutes

For each skewer you will need

FOR THE MARINADE (Sufficient for 4 skewers)
2 tablespoons olive oil
3 tablespoons soy sauce
3 tablespoons rum

FOR THE SKEWER
3 2-inch cubes veal
2 1-inch cubes cheese
2 thick slices green pepper
salt
paprika

FOR THE MARINADE
Mix all the ingredients together.

FOR THE SKEWER
Add veal to marinade and set aside for at least 2 hours. Thread the marinated veal on to the skewer and grill, about 4 inches from the hot fire, for about 18 minutes. Wrap the cheese cubes in the pepper slices, thread on to the end of the skewer and toast for the final 2 or 3 minutes. Sprinkle with salt and paprika and serve with Spiked Mixed Vegetables (see page 130).

BEEF AND BACON GRILL

Preparation time 15 minutes
Cooking time about 15 minutes
To serve 4

You will need

1½ lb. raw minced beef
2 teaspoons grated onion
½ teaspoon Worcestershire sauce
pinch pepper
½ teaspoon salt
4 rashers bacon, de-rinded, halved and rolled
8 small tomatoes
4 chicken livers
4 very small onions, parboiled
4 1½-inch cubes cooked sweet potato
2 oz. butter, melted
½ teaspoon chopped thyme
½ teaspoon chopped parsley
½ teaspoon chopped chives

Mix the minced beef, grated onion and Worcester-shire sauce. Season with pepper and salt, and roll into eight small balls. Flatten with a fork, marking both sides. Cook under a hot grill or over a fire for 5 minutes on each side.
If space allows, cook the bacon rolls, tomatoes, chicken livers, onions and potato cubes all brushed with melted butter at the same time; if there is not room, fry them separately.

Beef and bacon grill

Grease the skewers and thread with alternate ingredients allowing two meat balls, two bacon rolls and two tomatoes to each skewer. Brush with remaining melted butter, mixed with herbs and re-heat under the grill or over the fire. Place on long, halved slices of French bread and serve with mustard and plantain crisps (see page 17) or potato crisps.
Note
This is a good recipe for a lot of people. It can be prepared in advance in the kitchen, the skewers threaded and reheated when required.

TURKEY STEAKS

I was served these oyster skewers in Trinidad, but in my opinion, tree oysters are best eaten raw, exactly as one eats any other oysters. Old people in Port-of-Spain can remember the days when oysters were 4 cents a dozen and an old Chinaman came twice a day with his basket, patiently opening the oysters. Every member of a large family had 2 dozen oysters each day. Now, although the mangrove swamps around the rivers still yield these delicious molluscs, the price is no longer within everyone's reach.

Preparation time about 5 minutes
Cooking time about 5 minutes

For each skewer you will need

3 – 4 oysters, drained
2 rashers bacon, de-rinded and halved
strained juice ½ lime
½ teaspoon chopped chives

Wrap the oysters in bacon and grill until the bacon is crisp and the oysters begin to curl at the edges. Sprinkle with the lime juice, mixed with chives.

VARIATION
An alternative oyster skewer is made by rolling the oysters in breadcrumbs, or crumbs mixed with grated cheese. Oysters can alternate with cubes of ham on the skewer if preferred.

Lamchi and boonchi

LAMCHI AND BOONCHI

This skewer recipe is from the Dutch Antilles, as the name suggests.

Preparation time   7 minutes, plus overnight
                     marinating
Cooking time   15 – 20 minutes

For each skewer you will need

FOR THE MARINADE (Sufficient for 4 skewers)
strained juice 2 limes
2 tablespoons olive oil
1 onion, grated
1 tablespoon curry powder
1 chilli, de-seeded and chopped
2 teaspoons powdered ginger
2 teaspoons chopped turmeric
1 clove garlic, crushed
1 teaspoon salt
pinch cayenne pepper

FOR THE SKEWER
4 2-inch cubes lamb
½ slice pineapple, halved
1 rasher bacon, de-rinded and halved
2 thick slices green pepper

FOR THE MARINADE
Mix all the ingredients together.

FOR THE SKEWERS
Add lamb cubes to the marinade and set aside overnight. Thread skewer with alternate pieces of mari-

nated lamb, pineapple quarters and bacon wrapped around pepper slices. Brush once with marinade mixture and grill on a rack about 3 inches from the fire for 15 – 20 minutes, turning to brown on all sides. Serve with Peanut Sauce (see page 28).

SPIKED MIXED VEGETABLES

Preparation time   15 minutes, plus 4 hours
                     marinating
Cooking time   about 10 – 12 minutes

For each skewer you will need

2 tablespoons olive oil
½ clove garlic, crushed
4 1-inch cubes aubergine
2 wedges tomato
2 1-inch cubes yam, parboiled
1 small onion, parboiled
2 thick slices green pepper
½ oz. butter, melted

Put oil and garlic into a bowl, add aubergine and marinate for 4 hours. Drain. Thread aubergine, tomato, yam, onion and pepper on to a skewer alternately. Brush with butter and cook, about 3 inches from a slow fire, turning and basting with butter, for 10 – 12 minutes.
Note
Potato may be substituted for yam and any vegetable may be used; most require either marinating or parboiling.

CARNIVAL KEBABS

Preparation time   3 – 4 minutes
Cooking time   10 minutes

For each skewer you will need

3 2-inch cubes rump steak
2 very small tomatoes
2 chunks peeled pineapple
2 2-inch rings green pepper
2 eschalot or spring onion bulbs
½ oz. butter, melted
pinch chopped thyme
pinch chopped parsley
pinch chopped chives

Thread steak, tomatoes, pineapple, pepper rings, folded in half, and eschalots or spring onions on to a skewer alternately so that it looks attractive. Brush with melted butter, mixed with herbs and grill for 10 minutes, about 3 inches from the fire. Serve with Steak Sauce (see opposite).

INDONESIAN SKEWERED PORK

The skewers were cooked over wood smoke in Surinam where I first tried this dish.

Preparation time 10 – 15 minutes, plus 2 hours marinating
Cooking time 10 – 15 minutes
To serve 4 – 6

You will need

FOR THE MARINADE
6 oz. salted peanuts, finely minced
2 tablespoons coriander seeds, minced
2 cloves garlic, minced
1 chilli, de-seeded and crushed
2 onions, finely chopped
3 tablespoons lime juice
1 oz. dark brown sugar
4 tablespoons soy sauce
½ teaspoon pepper
4 oz. butter
¾ pint (U.S. 2 cups) chicken stock (see page 21)

FOR THE SKEWERS
2 lb. lean pork, cut into 1½-inch cubes

FOR THE MARINADE
Mix peanuts, coriander, garlic, chilli, onions, lime juice, sugar and soy sauce, season with pepper to taste and pound to a smooth pulp (a blender or food mill does the job well). Put the paste in a saucepan, bring to the boil, stir in butter and stock, cooking only until butter melts.

FOR THE SKEWERS
Marinate the meat cubes in this mixture for 2 hours, then thread on to skewers and grill on all sides until brown, basting with the marinade, mixed with the pan drippings. Serve on a bed of rice and chopped vegetables with the remaining marinade poured over the meat.

BARBECUE SAUCE FOR STEAK

Preparation time 7 minutes
Cooking time 15 minutes
To serve 6 – 8

You will need

¼ pint (U.S. ⅔ cup) peanut oil
3 tablespoons vinegar
scant ½ pint (U.S. 1 cup) boiling water
2 tablespoons Worcestershire sauce
2 small onions, pounded
2 chillis, de-seeded and finely chopped
1 clove garlic, grated
1 tablespoon brown sugar
1 tablespoon dry mustard
1 teaspoon salt
1 teaspoon paprika
1 teaspoon chopped thyme
1 teaspoon chopped sage
1 teaspoon chopped parsley
1 teaspoon chopped chives
dash Tabasco sauce

Put all the ingredients in a saucepan, mix well and cook over a low heat for 15 minutes. Brush steaks with this sauce before cooking and use as a baste during cooking. Refrigerated it will keep for a fortnight.

Barbecue sauce for steak

BARBECUE SAUCE FOR CHICKEN OR TURKEY

Preparation time 12 minutes
To serve 6 – 8

You will need

½ pint (U.S. 1¼ cups) strained orange juice
3 tablespoons strained lime juice
2 oz. butter, melted
3 tablespoons chopped parsley
1 tablespoon dry mustard
1 clove garlic, pounded
3 tablespoons soy sauce
3 tablespoons honey
salt

Blend all the ingredients together except the salt, which should be added just before serving. Use the sauce to brush the bird before cooking and as a baste during cooking.

LONG BAY PRAWNS IN MELON

Preparation time about 20 minutes
To serve 4 – 6

You will need

1 medium-sized melon
4 oz. peeled prawns
¼ pint (U.S. ⅔ cup) mayonnaise (see page 88)
1 tablespoon tomato ketchup
4½ tablespoons single cream
dash Tabasco sauce
1 small green pepper, de-seeded and chopped
pinch salt and pepper
1 tablespoon chopped tarragon

Slice the top off the melon. Scoop out the seeds and the flesh to within about ¾-inch from the rind. Put the melon shell and prawns to chill in the refrigerator. Mix the mayonnaise, tomato ketchup, cream, Tabasco and chopped pepper and season very lightly with salt and pepper. Cut the scooped-out melon flesh into cubes or balls, using a potato baller. Chill the sauce and melon cubes or balls and when everything is cold, mix and fill the melon shell. Serve chilled, sprinkled with tarragon.

LINDA ALLEYNE'S HAM MOUSSE

Preparation time 20 – 25 minutes
To serve 4 – 6

You will need

½ pint (U.S. 1¼ cups) aspic jelly
1 green pepper, de-seeded and cut in rings
8 oz. finely minced cooked lean ham or bacon
½ pint (U.S. 1¼ cups) white sauce (see page 28)
good pinch cayenne pepper
salt (optional)
½ pint (U.S. 1¼ cups) double cream, lightly whipped

Pour a ¼-inch layer of aspic jelly into the bottom of an oiled soufflé dish and leave to set. When set, arrange most of the pepper rings on top and pour over a little more aspic. Allow to set. Pound the minced ham, stir in the sauce and rub the mixture through a fine sieve or put into a blender. Season with cayenne and salt, if required. When the remaining aspic is just starting to set, mix into the ham, then carefully fold in the cream. Turn in to the soufflé dish and chill until set. Turn out and place remaining pepper rings, cut in half, round the base.

VARIATIONS
Chicken or lobster can be used instead of ham.

Linda Alleyne's ham mousse

EDAM FISH CHEESE

Preparation time 15 – 20 minutes
Cooking time 25 minutes
Oven temperature 375°F., Gas Mark 5
To serve 4 – 6

You will need

1 lb. cooked fish, boned and flaked
1 hard-boiled egg, finely chopped
salt and pepper
¼ teaspoon powdered thyme
½ pint white sauce (see page 28)
1 Edam cheese, 5 – 6 inches high

Add fish, egg, thyme and seasoning to sauce. Slice off the top of the cheese and scoop out most of the cheese inside, leaving about ¾-inch round the edge. Take great care not to break the shell. Tightly fill with the fish mixture, replace top, wrap in foil and bake in a moderately hot oven for about 25 minutes.

HOT MINCED CHICKEN SANDWICH

Preparation time 5 minutes
Cooking time 5 minutes
To serve 4

You will need

8 oz. finely minced cooked chicken
1 green pepper, de-seeded and chopped
2 teaspoons chopped chives
2 teaspoons chopped parsley
4½ tablespoons white sauce (see page 28)
¼ teaspoon black pepper
½ teaspoon salt
8 slices bread, toasted and buttered with crusts removed

Combine chicken, pepper, herbs, sauce and seasoning in a saucepan and mix well. Put over a gentle heat and when hot, spread on four slices of hot toast. Top with the other four slices. Cut in half diagonally and serve with lettuce, tomato quarters and cucumber.
Note
Any minced left-over meat or poultry is suitable for this type of hot toasted sandwich.

Banana toasts

BANANA TOASTS

Preparation time 8 minutes
Cooking time 8 minutes
To serve 4

You will need

2 eggs, beaten
4½ tablespoons milk
8 slices bread, crusts removed
2 oz. butter
3 large bananas, peeled and thinly sliced
2 teaspoons strained lime juice
2 tablespoons dark brown sugar
4 tablespoons warmed rum

On a large dinner plate, combine the egg and milk, and dip in the bread slices to coat on both sides. Heat the butter and fry the bread until pale golden, shaking the pan and turning. Drain, and cover one side of four slices with the banana rounds. Sprinkle with lime juice, top with a slice of bread, press down and sprinkle with sugar. Fry again just long enough to heat the filling and seal the sandwich. Cut sandwiches in half diagonally and pour over the rum.

BARBECUED BANANAS

Use firm, but not over-ripe, bananas. Slit skins along one side and grill in the skins until charred and soft. Open out the skins to use as a plate and serve with lime slices and a sprinkling of rum and sugar.

THE ISLES OF JUNE FRUIT SALAD

Preparation time 25 – 30 minutes
Cooking time 8 minutes
To serve 6 – 8

You will need

1 large cantaloup melon
3 large bananas
juice 1 lime
2 tangerines or canned mandarin oranges
1 small pawpaw
2 mangoes (optional)
1½ oz. castor sugar
1 tablespoon white rum
12 oz. strawberries, hulled
8 garden cherries, halved and stoned (optional)

FOR THE DRESSING
5 tablespoons strained orange juice
1 tablespoon strained lime juice
2 oz. castor sugar
2 egg yolks
¼ pint (U.S. ⅔ cup) single cream

Slash the melon down the section lines, but do not cut through to the base. Carefully open it out like a flower and scoop out a little of the flesh and the seeds. Drain off the juice and reserve it. Refrigerate the melon without allowing it to become too cold as this destroys the flavour.

Peel and slice the bananas and dip in lime juice to preserve the colour. Peel tangerines, if used, removing all the white pith. Cut into segments and remove pips. Cut pawpaw in half, remove seeds and dice flesh. If using mangoes, peel, remove stones and slice. Strain the melon juice, mix with the sugar, add the rum and blend well. Set aside a few strawberries for decorating, add the prepared fruit together with part, or all, the scooped-out melon to the sweetened juice and chill.

FOR THE DRESSING
Put the orange and lime juice in the top of a double boiler. Add the sugar and cook for about 3 minutes until the sugar dissolves, stirring all the time until very hot. Remove from the heat and allow the juice to cool slightly then add the egg yolks, one at a time and beating continuously. Replace the mixture over the bottom saucepan and cook over boiling water, stirring all the time from the bottom of the pan, until the sauce is thick and creamy. Allow to cool and when cold, beat in the cream and chill. Just before serving, fill the melon with some of the fruit salad and put the remainder round the base. Pour over enough juice to moisten but do not make it too wet. Decorate in between the melon slices with reserved strawberries. Serve the dressing separately or spoon over the fruit round the base.

FRUIT RISOTTO

(Illustrated in colour on page 135)

Preparation time 15 – 20 minutes, plus chilling time
Cooking time about 25 minutes
To serve 6

You will need

8 oz. rice
scant ½ pint (U.S. 1 cup) milk
scant ½ pint (U.S. 1 cup) water
3 oz. castor sugar
1 – 2 lb. fruit
¼ pint (U.S. ⅔ cup) double cream, lightly whipped (optional)

Cook rice in milk and water until nearly tender, then add 2 oz. sugar and continue cooking until it is quite tender and liquid absorbed. Drain and cool, then chill for 10 minutes. Cover bottom of a glass bowl with rice and top with a layer of dry, unsweetened fruit. Sprinkle lightly with sugar, cover with rice. Pile remaining fruit on top, sprinkle with sugar and coat with whipped cream, if liked.

Note
This dish can be made with just one fruit or a mixture of fruits. Strawberries, as illustrated, are plentiful in Jamaica.

Fruit risotto

Salt fish and ackee

REGIONAL RECIPES

This chapter is reserved for the regional dishes, the food of the islanders themselves. Not all can be made throughout the world and the average tourist will not often find them on hotel menus.

Some recipes had literally to be translated, the sort of instruction I was given ran on these lines: "So, ma'am, you takes a handful of peas, you strips dem peppers an' you cooks 'em jus' as dey wanna be cooked". Quantities too were vague. "You takes a likkle water liquid and a likkle lime juice", while timing was invariably "Until dey cooked". I found it better to watch rather than listen, but one evening in the Windward Islands, "Telephone want you", I was told, and off I went to see what the newly in-

stalled telephone had to say. "Man, I got a real good one, dis one blow up de jetty". I have *not* included this particular hot little number because, when tested, it proved too fiery for any but a few hardy West Indian palettes.

Names alone are exciting, French and Spanish rendered down for the English tongue. Most of the Indian recipes come from Trinidad and Guyana where Moslem mosques and Hindu temples are as numerous as churches. Even if they cannot be made away from the islands, even if they fail to tempt, these are the dishes with the true flavour of the islands.

SALT FISH AND ACKEE (Jamaica)

(Illustrated in colour on page 136)

Preparation time about 10 – 15 minutes
Cooking time about 30 minutes.
To serve 4

You will need

1 lb. soaked salt fish (see page 50)
18 ackees
4 rashers streaky bacon
1 large onion, thinly sliced
1 green pepper, de-seeded and sliced
4 tablespoons oil or 2 oz. butter
black pepper

Just cover salt fish with fresh cold water and bring to the boil. Remove pods, seeds and centres from ackees, tie in a muslin bag, add to the boiling fish and cook for 15 minutes, drain. Flake fish, discarding the skin and bone. Fry the bacon, remove and keep hot. Sauté the onion and pepper rings in the bacon fat, drain and keep hot with the bacon. In the same pan, heat the oil or butter, add the fish and ackees and heat through. Turn on to a heated dish and garnish with bacon, onion and pepper rings. Serve hot with plenty of black pepper. This is a national dish in Jamaica.

RED PEAS SOUP (Jamaica)

Preparation time 5 minutes, plus overnight
                                  soaking
Cooking time about 3 hours
To serve 4

You will need

8 oz. red 'peas' (kidney beans)
4 oz. salt pork or fat bacon
1 medium-sized onion, chopped
1 carrot, peeled and chopped
½ bay leaf
3 peppercorns
2 pints boiling water
salt and pepper

Cover the 'peas' with cold water and leave overnight, drain. Fry pork or bacon in a thick pan for about 5 minutes to extract the fat. Add the onion and the carrot and cook for a further 5 minutes, shaking the pan. Add 'peas', bay leaf, peppercorns and boiling water. Stir, cover and simmer for about 2½ hours or until 'peas' are soft. Remove pork or bacon and chop. Sieve 'peas' and liquid. Season to taste with salt and pepper, reheat and stir in chopped pork and bacon.

SALT FISH SOUSSE (Carriacou)

Carriacou is the largest of the Grenadine islands, and also the furthest South. It is very near to Grenada and is administered from there. An air strip was opened in 1968, making this pleasant little island more accessible, but for many, the schooner is still the most enjoyable way of reaching Carriacou.

Preparation time 7 – 10 minutes
To serve 4

You will need

1 onion, grated
1 chilli, de-seeded and minced
3 tablespoons olive oil
pinch salt
1 lb. cooked salt fish, finely flaked (see page 50)

TO GARNISH
1 green pepper, de-seeded and cut into strips
1 lettuce

Crush the onion and chilli with a fork and mix with the olive oil. Add the salt (use very little as the fish may still be salty) and fish and mix well. Garnish with strips of green pepper and serve on a bed of lettuce.

STAMP AND GO (Jamaica)

Preparation time 10 minutes
Cooking time 5 – 8 minutes
To serve 6

You will need

2 lb. plain flour and 4 teaspoons baking powder
    or 2 lb. self-raising flour
2 onions, grated
2 chillis, de-seeded and finely chopped
4 oz. butter or margarine, melted
½ pint (U.S. 1¼ cups) water
1 lb. cooked salt fish, finely flaked (see page 50)
deep fat or oil for frying

Sift the flour with the baking powder, if used. Add onions, chillis and butter or margarine and mix to a paste with water; use a little more water if the paste is too firm. When quite smooth, stir in the fish. Drop from a spoon into hot fat or oil and fry until the balls are golden brown. Drain and serve very hot.
Note
Some Jamaican recipes add 'annotto colouring' to this typical recipe, but this merely colours the fish balls slightly and is not necessary for the flavour.

CRAB BACKS (Trinidad)

Preparation time 10 – 15 minutes
Cooking time 40 minutes
Oven temperature 400°F., Gas Mark 6
To serve 4

You will need

8 live crabs
2 oz. butter
1 onion, finely chopped
2 teaspoons chopped chives
1 tablespoon Worcestershire sauce
salt and pepper
crisp breadcrumbs (raspings)

Put the crabs in a large pan and pour boiling water over to scald them, drain. Wash crabs, cover with fresh water, bring to the boil and cook for 30 minutes, by which time the flesh will be loosened. Remove the claws, prise them open and pick out the meat. Discard the gall clinging to the shell, remove meat and then scrub the shells.

Heat half the butter and brown the onion and chives. Add the flaked crab meat, Worcestershire sauce and salt and pepper. Refill the shells, sprinkle with breadcrumbs, dot with remaining butter and brown in a moderately hot oven for 10 minutes.

Note

Crabs are dirty feeders and should be kept for at least a day before cooking, feeding them on grass, bread and pepper leaves, until they are purged.

This dish is known as Baker Crab in Jamaica.

ESCOVITCH FISH (Jamaica)

Preparation time   7 – 10 minutes
Cooking time   about 25 minutes
To serve   4

You will need

4 green peppers, de-seeded and sliced in rings
4 onions, finely sliced
4 cooked carrots, sliced
2 bay leaves
3 tablespoons olive oil
$\frac{1}{4}$ pint (U.S. $\frac{2}{3}$ cup) vinegar
2 teaspoons salt
1 teaspoon pepper
$\frac{1}{2}$ pint (U.S. $1\frac{1}{4}$ cups) water
4 fillets white fish

Put the peppers, reserving a few slices for garnishing, onions, and carrots in a saucepan with the bay leaves, 1 tablespoon olive oil, vinegar, seasoning and water. Mix well, bring to the boil, and simmer over a low heat for 25 minutes. Brush the fish with the remaining oil and grill lightly on both sides. Put on a heated platter and pour the sauce over, first removing the bay leaves. Garnish with reserved pepper rings.

Note

If liked, the sauce can be thickened with 1 tablespoon flour.

RUN DOWN (Jamaica)

Many of the dishes cooked in coconut milk have this type of name like 'Run Down' and 'Oiled Down' which is doubtless due to the oil in the coconut milk.

Preparation time   10 – 15 minutes
Cooking time   30 – 35 minutes
To serve   4 – 5

You will need

12 oz. any small fish, such as mackerel, shad or crayfish or salt fish
$1\frac{1}{2}$ pints (U.S. $3\frac{3}{4}$ cups) coconut milk
1 onion, grated
2 green peppers, de-seeded and chopped
2 tomatoes, thinly sliced
1 clove garlic, crushed
2 teaspoons chopped thyme
2 teaspoons chopped chives
2 tablespoons vinegar
1 teaspoon salt
$\frac{3}{4}$ teaspoon black pepper

If salt fish is used, prepare and cook (see page 50) or bone fresh fish and cut into pieces. Boil the coconut milk and continue boiling until it becomes oily, about 15 minutes. Add the vegetables, herbs and seasonings and cook for a further 10 minutes, then add the fish and cook until tender.

Escovitch fish

Curried goat in a Ras Tafari's bowl

CURRIED GOAT (Jamaica)

This is almost a National Jamaican dish, eaten by many people at least once a week, even the Ras Tafaris, the sect who follow the Emperor of Ethiopia. The 'Rastas' make very durable cooking bowls from scrap aluminium, hand cast in sand. The aluminium is melted over a charcoal fire, poured into a mould and plugged after it hardens. One can put these bowls on the fire and they stay hot for a long time after removal, cold things stay cold and they can be hurled around and never break.

Preparation time 10 minutes, plus 1 hour marinating
Cooking time about 1 – 1½ hours
To serve 4

You will need

1½ lb. goat or mutton, trimmed and cut into 1 – inch cubes
1 teaspoon salt
1 teaspoon black pepper
1 tablespoon curry powder
1 oz. lard or other cooking fat
1 onion, sliced
½ pint (U.S. 1¼ cups) stock (see page 21) or water
2 chillis, de-seeded and chopped
2 English potatoes, peeled and diced

Season the meat with salt, pepper and curry powder, sifted together and rubbed into the cubes. Set aside for 1 hour. Heat the lard or fat in a saucepan, add the meat and onion and brown lightly. Add the stock or water and chillis, cover and simmer over a low heat until the meat is tender; the timing varies with the meat, mutton, which is more often used for 'curried goat', takes less time than goat. Add the potatoes and continue cooking for a further 20 minutes or until they are soft and the gravy thickens. Serve on a bed of rice.

SOUSE (Barbados)

This type of souse is served in other islands, but is typical of Barbados. I was given it as a first course in the sea, before a beach lunch in Tobago and it is a popular Saturday supper dish.

Preparation time about 20 minutes, plus 8 hours marinating
Cooking time about 1½ hours
To serve 4 – 6

You will need

½ pig's head
1 pig's tongue
2 pig's trotters
salt
strained juice 6 limes
1 cucumber, peeled and sliced
1 small onion, minced

TO GARNISH
sprig parsley

Scald the meats in boiling water and scrape the head meat from the bone with a sharp knife. Wash in salted water and the juice of 2 limes. Tie the meats in a clean cloth, put into cold water and bring to the boil. Simmer over a low heat for 1½ hours. Remove the meat and plunge into cold water. Untie it, skin the tongue and slice it, slice the head meat and split and skin the trotters. Put all the sliced meat into a deep dish, sprinkle with 1 tablespoon salt and juice of about 2 limes. Just cover with cold water and set aside to marinate for 8 hours. Soak cucumber in salted water for 15 minutes, drain. Make a sauce with the remaining lime juice, salt, onion, cucumber and ¼ pint (U.S. ⅔ cup) of the meat stock, well mixed and chilled. When the meat is marinated, drain it and serve covered with sauce and garnished with parsley. Serve with Pudding (see opposite).

PUDDING (Barbados)

Pudding stems directly from the Scottish exiles, banished after the Monmouth Rebellion, or, as the saying was 'Barbadosed'.

Preparation time 20 minutes, plus 1 hour
soaking
Cooking time about $1\frac{1}{4} - 1\frac{1}{2}$ hours
To serve 4 – 6

You will need

pig's intestines, about 2 yards in all
salt
lime juice
4 large sweet potatoes, peeled and grated
3 – 4 eschalots or spring onions, finely
chopped
2 teaspoons chopped thyme
about 1 teaspoon cayenne pepper
1 tablespoon chopped marjoram
2 oz. butter or margarine
$\frac{1}{4}$ teaspoon powdered cloves
1 tablespoon brown sugar
water to bind

Turn the intestines inside out and clean them thoroughly with salt and lime juice. Soak them in salted water, to which lime juice has been added, for 1 hour. Mix all the other ingredients, add salt and bind with a little water to a crumbly paste. Cut the soaked intestines into 8-inch lengths, fill loosely with the mixture and tie at each end. Put into the top of a steamer and steam slowly for about 50 minutes, pricking the skins after 30 minutes to prevent bursting. This pudding is usually served with Souse (see opposite).

Note
For black pudding, add pig's blood to binding water.

OILED DOWN (Grenada)

When I was first offered this dish, it sounded unattractive, but cooked in the Grenadian way it is delicious.

Preparation time 15 minutes, plus overnight
soaking
Cooking time about 45 – 50 minutes
To serve 4 – 6

You will need

8 oz. salt meat
1 large or 2 small breadfruit, cut into 4 or 6
sections
8 oz. cooked salt fish, flaked (see page 50)
1 whole chilli
2 sprigs thyme
2 chives
1 stick celery, chopped or $\frac{1}{2}$ teaspoon celery
seeds
$2\frac{3}{4}$ pints (U.S. 7 cups) coconut milk
salt

Soak meat overnight in cold water, drain. Remove the breadfruit core and peel. In a saucepan, put alternate layers of breadfruit, meat and fish. Tie chilli, thyme and chives together and add to the pan with the celery and coconut milk. Cover tightly and bring to the boil, reduce heat and simmer for about 45 – 50 minutes until everything is cooked and tender. When cooked the liquid should all be absorbed and the stew oily. Remove herbs before serving and add salt to taste.

FRIED MOUNTAIN CHICKEN (Dominica)

Preparation time 10 minutes, plus 2 hours
marinating
Cooking time about 8 – 10 minutes
To serve 4

You will need

8 pairs frogs' legs
$\frac{1}{4}$ pint (U.S. $\frac{2}{3}$ cup) vinegar
2 tablespoons salt
$\frac{1}{2}$ teaspoon pepper
1 oz. butter
1 tablespoon strained lime juice
1 teaspoon finely chopped parsley

Wash and dry frogs' legs. Mix vinegar and salt and marinate legs in this mixture for 2 hours. Spoon liquid over legs several times while marinating. Drain and dry and season with pepper. Heat butter and sauté legs on both sides until golden brown. Serve sprinkled with lime juice and chopped parsley.
Note
Mountain chicken are very large frogs found and bred in mountainous Dominica where this dish is a speciality. The flavour is very like poussin.

Jug-Jug

JUG-JUG (Barbados)

'Jug' is a Bajan Christmas speciality, served with turkey. Jug-Jug came to Barbados, like Pudding (see page 141) via the Scottish 17th Century exiles, in an attempt to produce something resembling haggis.

Preparation time	about 20 – 25 minutes, plus overnight soaking for salt meat
Cooking time	about 1¼ hours
To serve	4 – 6

You will need

8 oz. fresh or salt pork
8 oz. fresh or salt beef
1½ pints (U.S. 3¾ cups) water
pepper
1 lb. pigeon peas
1 tablespoon chopped thyme
1 tablespoon chopped parsley
1 tablespoon chopped chives
1 onion, minced
4 oz. guinea corn
2 oz. butter

Soak salt pork and beef overnight in cold water, drain. Cut up the meat. Cook the pork for 20 minutes with the water, then add the beef, season with pepper to taste and add the peas. Cook for a further 25 – 30 minutes until the peas are soft. Strain and retain half the stock. Mince the meat finely, add the peas and pound in a mortar until a smooth purée is obtained, or put in an electric blender. Meanwhile add the herbs and onion to the reserved stock and boil for about 5 minutes, then slowly add the guinea corn, stirring briskly for 10 minutes. Add the meat and pea purée and cook over a low heat for a further 20 minutes. Stir in 1½ oz. butter, transfer to a heated crock tied with a clean napkin and top with the rest of the butter.

Note
It is *not* the custom, but I find Jug-Jug delicious if eaten with crisp toast, like pâté, but rather too rich to be enjoyed as a side dish. Every Barbadian cook has a different recipe, all vary according to tradition in that particular family, but this is the basic, and most usual method. Barbadians living overseas tell me they find porridge oats a good substitute for guinea corn, which is not cornflour, but something like whole-wheat flour.

ROTI (Trinidad and Guyana)

Stalls selling roti, or little roadside barrows, are a common sight all through Trinidad.

Preparation time	10 minutes
Cooking time	about 10 minutes
To make	8 roti

You will need

8 oz. plain flour
½ teaspoon bicarbonate of soda
pinch salt
4 – 5 tablespoons milk
ghee (see page 31)

Sift flour, bicarbonate of soda and salt and bind with enough milk to make a stiff dough. With floured hands, roll into balls about the size of an egg, flatten and spread with ghee, then pat back to the egg shape again. Flatten once more and cook on a hot griddle turning frequently during cooking, brushing with ghee. Spread well with ghee and clap together between both hands, covered by a clean cloth.

Note
Roti made with ghee are called *Paratha*, but more popular in the islands are those with spiced or curried meat inside, instead of the last spreading of ghee. In Jamaica, they are called patties.

Piononos

PIONONOS (Puerto Rico)

This recipe comes from La Fonda del Callejòn in Old San Juan where the food is a delicious mixture of Caribbean ingredients prepared in the Spanish manner. One eats in a cool courtyard and upstairs is a museum showing how mid-19th century Puerto Rican families lived.

Preparation time 10 – 15 minutes
Cooking time about 25 – 30 minutes
To serve 4

You will need

2 ripe plantains, peeled and cut lengthways into four strips
1 oz. butter
1 egg, lightly beaten
corn oil for frying

FOR THE FILLING
12 oz. minced raw beef
2 oz. minced cooked ham
1 small green pepper, de-seeded and minced
1 onion, minced
1 large or 2 small tomatoes, skinned and chopped
1½ tablespoons olive oil
½ teaspoon salt
¼ teaspoon pepper

Fry the plantains in butter until tender, about 7 minutes. Curve the slices into rings and secure with cocktail sticks.

FOR THE FILLING
Blend all the ingredients for the meat filling, and fry over a low heat until the meat is cooked, about 20 minutes. Pack the meat into the plantain rings, brush both sides with egg and fry in hot corn oil for a few minutes.

RICE AND PEAS (Jamaica)

This is the simplest form of rice and peas, the 'Jamaican Coat of Arms', sometimes bacon, salt pork or stewing meat is added. In Jamaica, it is always called Rice and Peas although on some other islands it becomes Peas an' Rice. In the Bahamas, tomatoes are added and the dish is called Hoppin' John.

Preparation time 5 minutes, plus overnight soaking
Cooking time 45 – 50 minutes
To serve 4 – 6

You will need

8 oz. red 'peas' (kidney beans) or 'gungo' peas
pinch bicarbonate of soda (optional)
1½ pints (U.S. 3¾ cups) boiling water
1 pint (U.S. 2½ cups) coconut milk
2 teaspoons chopped thyme
2 eschalots or spring onions, finely chopped
1 chilli, de-seeded and chopped
salt and pepper
1 lb. rice

Soak 'peas' overnight in cold water with bicarbonate of soda, if liked, drain. Put the 'peas' in the fast boiling water and cook for about 25 minutes or until tender but still whole. Add the coconut milk, thyme, eschalots or spring onions, chilli, salt and pepper. Bring once again to boiling point and boil for 5 minutes. Add the rice, stir, cover and cook over a very low heat until the rice is tender and the liquid absorbed, about 20 minutes. Drain and serve very hot on a large platter.

COO-COO POIS (Carriacou)

Preparation time 7 – 10 minutes, plus overnight
soaking
Cooking time 1 hour 20 minutes
To serve 4

You will need

8 oz. dried peas
pinch bicarbonate of soda (optional)
3 pints (U.S. 7½ cups) water
8 oz. salt beef
1 lb. cornflour or conquintay flour
salt and pepper

Soak the peas overnight in cold water with bicarbonate of soda added, if liked, drain. Put the soaked
peas into 2¾ pints (U.S. 7 cups) water, bring slowly
to the boil, then add the meat and simmer until both
peas and meat are cooked, about 40 – 45 minutes.
Remove the meat and keep warm, add the cornflour or conquintay flour very slowly to the peas and
water, stirring vigorously with a coo-coo stick or
wooden spoon until there is a smooth paste, free
from lumps. Bring the rest of the water to the boil,
add to the paste and allow to stand for 10 minutes.
Stir and cook over a very low heat for a further 30
minutes. Season to taste and stir before serving with
the meat.
Note
Coo-coo, a derivation of *cook*, is different from the
cou-cou of Barbados.

FOO FOO (Barbados)

Preparation time 7 – 10 minutes
Cooking time about 30 minutes
To serve 4 – 6

You will need

4 – 5 green plantains
salt and pepper

Boil unpeeled plantains until soft, about 30 minutes
according to size. Allow to cool, then peel and
pound in a mortar dipping the pestle frequently into
water to prevent sticking. When a smooth ball forms,
reheat, season and serve with peppery soups. (Illustrated in black and white on page 22.)
Note
If liked, the foo foo can be rolled into small balls.

Dal

DAL (Trinidad and Guyana)

Preparation time 7 – 10 minutes, plus overnight
soaking
Cooking time 25 – 30 minutes
To serve 4

You will need

8 oz. dried split peas
pinch bicarbonate of soda (optional)
pinch saffron powder or 1 tablespoon curry
powder
½ teaspoon salt
1 small onion, finely chopped
1 tablespoon coconut oil
1 clove garlic, crushed

Soak the peas overnight in cold water, with
bicarbonate of soda added, if liked, drain.

Just cover the soaked split peas with fresh water, add
the saffron or curry powder and cook until the peas
are soft, about 20 – 25 minutes. Drain, add the salt
and onion and stir briskly. Heat the coconut oil and
fry the garlic for 3 – 4 minutes, remove the garlic
and add the flavoured oil to the split peas. Heat and
serve with rice.

CORN COU-COU (Barbados)

Cou-cou is Barbadian and most households serve
it every week. Children play a clapping game, 'Who
stole the cou-cou from the cou-cou pot?'

Preparation time 5 minutes
Cooking time 20 – 25 minutes
To serve 4

You will need

12 okras
2½ pints (U.S. 6¼ cups) water
1½ tablespoons salt
8 oz. cornmeal
1 oz. butter

Cut the stems off the okras and slice in rings. Add half the water to half the salt, bring to the boil, put in the okra rings and boil for 10 minutes. Sift the cornmeal, add it to the rest of the water and salt and mix thoroughly. Remove okras from the heat and stir in the cornmeal paste until well blended. Cook gently, stirring all the time for about a further 10 minutes or until the mixture becomes smooth and stiff and leaves the saucepan clean. Put into a heated dish and spread with butter. This dish is often served with flying fish.

GULGULA (Guyana)

Preparation time 10 minutes
Cooking time about 7 minutes
To make 12 slices

You will need

1 lb. plain flour and 1 teaspoon baking powder
  or 1 lb. self-raising flour
1 teaspoon ground mixed spice
3 eggs
5 tablespoons milk
4 oz. stoned raisins
1 lb. brown sugar
deep fat or oil for frying

Sift the flour with baking powder, if used, and spice. Add the eggs and enough milk to make a stiff paste. Beat well and add raisins and half the sugar. Mix well, then turn on to a floured board and form into a roll. Divide into 1-inch slices, dust each slice with sugar and fry in hot fat or oil until cooked through and golden brown. Sprinkle again with sugar before serving hot or cold.

MATRIMONY (Jamaica)

Preparation time 8 – 10 minutes
To serve 4

You will need

4 star apples
3 oranges
¼ pint (U.S. ⅔ cup) double cream or evaporated
  milk
castor sugar
1 tablespoon rum (optional)

Scoop out the pulp from the apples and discard the pips. Peel 1 orange, leaving the pith, and cut 4 slices for decoration. Peel away the pith from the remainder and from the other two oranges. Divide into segments, remove pips and roughly chop. Mix the star apple pulp with the orange slices and mash well. Beat the cream or evaporated milk until thick and fold into the fruit mixture. Add sugar to taste, less sugar will be needed, if any, with the evaporated milk than with the cream. Add the rum if liked and serve chilled in individual glasses. Decorate with reserved orange slices.
Note
Star apples are large, dark skinned fruit with the pips in a star formation in the centre. Eaten alone they are rather tasteless but blended with orange, the result is cool and refreshing. Some cooks omit the rum and add a little grated nutmeg, but I prefer the recipe using the rum.

Matrimony

CONKIES (Barbados)

Conkies are made for Guy Fawkes Day and all through November, but no one seems to know exactly what is the origin of this custom.

Preparation time about 15 minutes
Cooking time   1 hour
To make   12 conkies

You will need

about 12 oz. peeled ripe coconut, grated
8 oz. pumpkin, peeled and grated
2 sweet potatoes, peeled and grated
12 oz. brown sugar
1 teaspoon powdered allspice
1 teaspoon grated nutmeg
1 teaspoon almond essence
4 oz stoned raisins (optional)
2 oz. flour
8 oz. freshly ground Indian corn or cornmeal
pinch salt
6 oz. butter or cooking fat, melted
½ pint (U.S. 1¼ cups) milk
almond, plantain or banana leaves, cut into
   8-inch squares

Mix coconut, pumpkin, potato, sugar, spices, almond essence, raisins, if used, flour, corn or cornmeal and salt. When well blended, add the melted butter or fat and milk and stir with a wooden spoon to a smooth paste.
Put 2 tablespoons of this mixture on to 12 cut leaves, fold the edges over to make a neat parcel and tie securely. Place conkies on a rack and steam in a large saucepan for 1 hour, covered with the same leaves with which the conkies are wrapped. Cut the threads and use the leaves as plates.

MOHAN BHOG (Trinidad)

This is the traditional Indian sweet cake made for special occasions with flour and rice flour in equal parts. To make the rice flour, white rice is steamed and dried in the sun. When quite dry, it is ground to a fine powder.

Preparation time 10 – 15 minutes
Cooking time   5 minutes
To make   8 slices

You will need

8 oz. plain flour
¼ teaspoon bicarbonate of soda
1 teaspoon powdered allspice
8 oz. castor sugar
4 oz. stoned raisins
about 5 tablespoons goat's milk or water
2 oz. ghee (see page 31)

In a heavy saucepan, shake the flour over a low heat, until it turns golden, then sift it with the soda, allspice and sugar. Add raisins. With the goat's milk or water, mix to a paste, which will drop from the end of a wooden spoon. Heat the ghee, stir in the flour mixture and continue stirring over a low heat until the ghee is absorbed, about 5 minutes. Allow the paste to cool, then shape into a cake and cut into slices when cold.

SORREL (various islands)

Preparation time 5 minutes, plus standing and
                    fermenting time
To make   6 pints (U.S. 15 cups)

You will need

3 lb. ripe sorrel
1-inch green ginger
1 – 2 pieces dried orange peel
12 cloves
6 pints (U.S. 15 cups) boiling water
barley or rice
2 lb. granulated sugar

Discard seeds, wash and put sorrel sepals (which are red when ripe) into a large crock or jar (use two if necessary). Add ginger, orange peel and cloves. Pour on boiling water, cover with a cloth and set aside for 24 hours. Strain, put a few grains of barley or rice into each bottle (this helps fermentation) and add sugar. Cork and leave overnight.

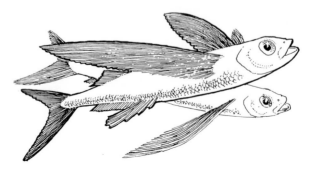

INDEX

ACKNOWLEDGEMENTS

The author gratefully acknowledges help received from air and shipping lines, from Tourist Boards and from her many friends throughout the islands.

The publishers wish to acknowledge the help of the following with photography: Casa Pupo, Derby Pottery, the Eastern Caribbean Tourist Board, Fyffes Group Ltd., the Jamaica Tourist Board, C. J. Newnes (Fishmongers) and Tropical Plants Display, Ltd.